MW00639828

MOVE

THE MAN DEVOTIONAL

Fedd Books
P.O. Box 341973
Austin, TX 78734

www.thefeddagency.com

Published in association with The Fedd Agency, Inc., a literary agency.

ISBN: 978-1-949784-25-1
eISBN: 978-1-949784-26-8

Printed in the United States of America

First Edition 15 14 13 12 11 / 10 9 8 7 6 5 4 3 2

This book is dedicated to all the great men whose names are unknown and unwritten. They will never be on stage, followed on social media, or have their name in lights. But they get up every day, put on their boots, and faithfully hit the same nail. They are the foundation stones that help build my faith, and I hope this book helps you join them.

As you come to him, the living Stone—rejected by humans but chosen by God and precious to him—you also, like living stones, are being built into a spiritual house to be a holy priesthood, offering spiritual sacrifices acceptable to God through Jesus Christ.

- 1 Peter 2:4-5

TABLE OF CONTENTS

INTRODUCTION

THROUGHOUT THE BIBLE, GOD IS REPEATEDLY referred to as "Father." For a long time, that image didn't help me because my dad and I are very different. I'm over six feet, he is under six feet. I had bad grades at a low-grade college, he was on the Dean's List at multiple Ivy League schools. He loves James Bond, I prefer Thor. He has never finished a beer, I'll drink multiple beers in the same sitting. His job is troubleshooting nuclear reactors, I have a hard time troubleshooting my motorcycle. He has never had tobacco, I love tobacco in nearly every form.

I came to the conclusion that my dad isn't like me and doesn't understand me. Believing this caused distance in our relationship. And for a long time, I felt the same way about my Heavenly Father. I was driven away from God and there was a barrier in my relationship with Him because I thought He had nothing in common with me and therefore couldn't understand me. I now know that He does understand me, and He even likes me. But not every man has come to that conclusion.

I believe it's hard for men to get to know God because we don't know how to spend time with Him. Much of what helps other people spend time with God doesn't help me. Maybe that's because I'm a man, and there isn't much on the market written with me in mind. It's no secret that the vast majority of churchgoers are women, and preachers consciously or unconsciously speak to their core audience. It's well known in the publishing industry that 80 percent of books are bought by women, whether Christian or not. Even a recent book I wrote for men called *The Five Marks of a Man* has been purchased by more women than men. It is likely that a woman in your life bought this book for you. That's a smart woman. Please thank her on my behalf.

I'm a fifty-three-year-old man who has been walking with God for thirty-seven years. Over that span of time, I've learned a lot and taken my share of punches. As I've aged, things that I've shared on the back deck or around a campfire have often proved helpful in many lives. Those lessons are recorded in this book and they come directly out of the Bible and have been verified by my life experience.

Contained in this book are sixty-six readings that will help men in their understanding of God, which will result in having more strength to lead a life that works. Not all of these devotions will be immediately applicable to every man. But I can promise you that there is something here for every man looking to operate with spiritual power in a life that is moving in the right direction. Some sections will be incredibly invigorating and others unduly offensive. I'm talking to you the way I would if you were with me on that back deck or around that campfire. If it is helpful, great. If not, set it aside.

For each reading, I'll give you a verse, some teaching on that verse, a prayer you can pray, and then actual tactile things you can do if you want to get off your spiritual couch and get your rear into gear. It is what you *do* that defines your relationship with God, not what you think or feel. Jesus says that you know a tree by its fruit, not its feelings. This book is written to push, challenge, and spark you into movement. By opening these pages, you're inviting God to push you. If you don't want to move, you might as well put this down right now.

Still reading? Good. Most men I know want to move; they want to do things. Jesus didn't come to hold class; He came to change the world. He came to move you and me out of the place of apathy and into a place of challenge.

Some friends and I started an unfiltered and challenging experience designed to move men to a new place spiritually. Over the last few years, I've spoken to and camped with fifteen thousand men from around the country at this thing called "Man Camp." Man Camp is for a specific type of guy. There is a kind of guy who doesn't understand "church speak," but when spoken to directly about spiritual things, he responds. There is a kind of guy who has no room in his schedule or his mind for theological philosophies. There is a kind of guy who wants to build a fully engaged life—physically, mentally, *and* spiritually—instead of just having some spirituality on the side. This was the vision for Man Camp, and it is the vision for the book you are holding.

There is something special that happens when men are with men who want to move to the next level. I've seen a fifty-year-old man put his hand on the shoulder of a twenty-year-old guy who was stressed about the future and say, "You are going to be fine. Stop wasting energy thinking about what could go wrong and put your energy into making things go right." I saw the stress drain from his face and shoulders. We need encouraging and helpful straight talk like this which is what this book is designed to give.

I was around one campfire when a guy started whining about how his wife was cheating on him. Another guy felt a prompting from God and said, "And how many women have you had sex with outside your marriage?" He was busted, and his life turned around that night with that straight talk. He went home and moved on his new convictions. He changed the way he treated his wife. He got off the spiritual couch and got into the game.

There is a level of realness, vulnerability, and playfulness with the right guys in the right setting that is a far cry from what often happens at church-sponsored events. I want to bring that realness, vulnerability, and playfulness to your life through the words in this book. I want to do it not for the fun of hitting some taboo topics, but rather for the joy of seeing you move. Following Jesus isn't a sedentary philosophical pursuit, it is something that requires physical engagement—you've gotta move.

It has been rather invigorating to write and self-publish this book without needing to have the approval of people I don't know who are sitting in an office in some other city and have never farted around a campfire. I'm not trying to win an award. Nor am I trying to be liked with this book. I'm just trying to help you to better know the God who created you and to live with strength and success. Your God wants you to move from the static lifestyle that most of us have fallen prey to.

Too many dudes have weak and anemic spiritual lives. I want more for you. I want your life to be different. I want you to finish every section of this book with fewer cobwebs in your mind. I want your future to be better because you are closer to God and more aware of His truth. You can have more power. I'm committed to helping you get there, and you will get there if you move on what is in the pages of this devotional. Let's get our rear in gear and start moving.

HEARING FROM GOD

And behold, a voice from heaven said, "This is my beloved Son, with whom I am well pleased."

- MATTHEW 3:17

I'VE BEEN BURNED BY RELIGIOUS PEOPLE WHO GIVE me a message they "heard from God." Often the message is negative, and they overplay their hand by implying that their eardrums picked up decibels sent from heaven.

But make no mistake about it: God is a God who speaks. I wish He spoke to me and other modern men like He did to some ancient men in the Bible, with a voice from heaven. When Jesus was baptized, Matthew tells us that He heard a voice from heaven. Was this an audible sound that rang in His ears? I don't think in this instance as there is no evidence that anyone else heard the Father's words to Jesus.

Sometime later, Jesus was with a few of His friends on a mountaintop, and God the Father shows up again—this time even more mystically and powerfully—in the form of a bright cloud. Matthew 17:5-6 explains that "A voice from the cloud said, 'This is my beloved Son, with whom I am well pleased; listen to him.' When the disciples heard this, they fell on their faces and were terrified." The frightened reaction of Jesus' friends makes it clear that God's voice here was audible—terrifying even.

I've never heard God with my eardrums, and I'm willing to bet you haven't either. I hope we all do eventually, but in the meantime, we most certainly can hear from God. When you read scriptures that God has preserved for millennia and which have helped millions of people, you are hearing from God. When a thought "randomly" crosses your mind, one you wouldn't normally generate and God would approve of, you are hearing from God. When you read something in this book that strikes you as important, you may be hearing from God.

There are many ways that God speaks to us, but there is only one way to encourage God to keep speaking to us: listen and respond to what He tells you by doing what He commands. And, God is a leader who doesn't just give instructions. He gives affirmations like, "I'm pleased with you. You are doing a good job!" He also gives coaching like, "You are working too hard. Do something fun this weekend."

There are sections in this book that will make you go, "meh." There are other sections that will smack you in the mouth. What speaks to one man might not speak to another. God is speaking to a man who means a lot to Him. You are His son, and He wants what's best for you, and He is telling you how to make that happen. Listen and follow through!

PRAYER

God, I want to hear from you. I don't want a religion that is an impersonal rule book. I want a relationship which brings communication. Please help me to develop my hearing as I listen for you. Amen.

GET MOVING

1. What is one area of your life that you'd like God to speak into over the next sixty-six days? Find a spot where you can talk out loud and ask Him, in your audible voice, to speak to you.
2. You don't have to wait to hear God's voice to do the right thing. Think of one thing you can do today that you know God would approve of. Then go do it.

DAY 02

WHAT IS IT YOU WANT?

And Jesus said to him, "What do you want me to do for you?"

- MARK 10:51

JESUS IS RECORDED ASKING THIS QUESTION ON MULtiple occasions. It isn't a trick question. It isn't rhetorical. He asks people, and He is asking you, "What do you want me to do for you?" Talk about winning the lottery. The Son of God, who performs miracles, asks you what you want. What do you say?

You may feel uncomfortable answering that question. Maybe you feel guilty that you already have so much; why should you ask for more when there are starving people in the world? You may feel this question sets you up for a televangelist moment where I tell you that blessings are going to shower down on your life if you send in a check. But remember, it's not me who's asking, it's Jesus, directly addressing *you* and your wants and needs.

Jesus asked this question to a man who was blind. Maybe the guy had bigger problems than his blindness and Jesus was offering to fix them. Maybe Jesus just wanted to hear him articulate his need to recover his sight. Either way, nothing was going to change in this guy's situation until he asked Jesus.

What do you want Jesus to do for you? You are important to Him. He cares about a man like you who is hanging with this book. A man who intentionally wants to get off his rear end and aggressively move toward a more challenging and meaningful life. It is because God is doing something special in your life and He wants to do more.

So, I'll ask you again, what do you want Jesus to do for you? I can feel emotion welling up inside of me because things are going to change as a result of what you pray next.

PRAYER

Jesus, I want you to ______________________ . Father, I ask that you say "yes" to this prayer. It is hard to believe that you want to do things for me. Help me to believe this as I ask and wait expectantly. Amen.

GET MOVING

1. Do you believe that God actually wants to do something for you? Jesus wouldn't ask if He wasn't serious. He genuinely knows you and cares for you.
2. Carve out two more times today where you can just stop and remind yourself that you are known by God Himself and tell Him thank you for wanting to show up in your life.

THE GRACE/TRUTH PARADOX

And the Word became flesh and dwelt among us, and we have seen his glory, glory as of the only Son from the Father, full of grace and truth.

-JOHN 1:14

A PARADOX IS WHEN TWO OPPOSING CONCEPTS ARE united to make one powerful truth. We believe grace and truth are opposed to one another, and yet their unity brings transcendent spiritual power. Truth is about reality regardless of the pain. Grace is about second chances and letting things slide. Truth is that when you lose your balance, gravity sucks. Grace is the mattress placed under you.

Most of us either fully embrace grace or fully embrace truth. Grace people are always willing to forgive, to a fault. Truth people cut you off after one misstep. Grace people try to understand a person who has bad beliefs. Truth people just give straight talk.

Grace people are okay with ambiguity. Truth people see everything fitting into a math equation.

Jesus doesn't operate just as truth or just as grace. He fully embodies both. The truth is that I'm a sinner who deserves eternal hell. The grace of Jesus enables me not only to escape that place but to abide in a fulfilling and lasting relationship with God. There were times when Jesus gave truth and there were times when He gave grace, but He refused to be pigeonholed in one category or the other. This was one reason why His life was so significant.

I encourage you to identify your default response to the stimuli in your life. We all err on the side of truth or grace. Personally, I'm more of a truth person. Knowing this, I spend more energy asking myself questions like, "How can I show grace to this person?" or, "What would be the grace-giving approach that Jesus would take?" If you are a grace person ask yourself, "What are the immutable laws that this person needs to be aware of?"

As of now, the only tattoo on my body is a grace/truth graphic on my left shoulder surrounded by a crown of thorns. It was on the cross that Jesus gave me grace in dying for me because the truth was that I was lost. I am committed to be a person who is marked by truth *and* grace. You should be too.

PRAYER

God, you astound me. How could someone so big and vast who knows and embodies all truth give grace to a sinner like me?! I want to be more like you to those who are around me. Today I'm going to practice the thing I'm not very good at. Please bring the right people across my path, who need grace when I would normally only give them truth, or vice versa. Amen.

GET MOVING

1. What is your default response to the people and situations in your life: truth or grace?
2. Identify one way that you can offer the other response today, especially if it is to someone you often dislike or disagree with.

DAY 04

IT IS A GREAT THING TO BE A MAN

Be strong, and show yourself a man, and keep the charge of the Lord your God, walking in his ways and keeping his statutes, his commandments, his rules, and his testimonies, as it is written in the Law of Moses, that you may prosper in all that you do and wherever you turn.

- 1 KINGS 2:2-3

IT PROBABLY WON'T SURPRISE YOU TO LEARN THAT I've never been a woman. If I were, I'm sure I would see amazing benefits of being a female. But since it's just us, let's dwell on the high calling of being a man.

Have you ever considered that it is a blessing to be a man? Practically, we get the ease of peeing standing up. Physically, we tend to have more body mass to get manual things done. Functionally, throughout history, we have had opportunities available to us that weren't available to women.

One of the craziest, most inspiring passages in

the Bible takes place when the great king David is on his deathbed. David calls his son Solomon, who is his successor, into his chambers for his final counsel. He doesn't tell him to be an enlightened individual or a mature adult, but to be a strong man. In some ways, this is freeing for us. Men should be men! Men should live out the blessing that's been given to them. But it is also a challenge. "Be strong," David says, "and show yourself a man" (1 Kings 2). Live up to that calling, he tells Solomon, and *prove* your manhood.

We men must acknowledge the unique blessings that have come our way and put them into play. You being a man is a gift you should not squander. Do what Solomon was instructed to do. Prove yourself a man by:

- Keeping God's mission for your life.
- Walking in God's ways.
- Prospering in whatever you do.

You have one life to lead. Make it count. Grab opportunities by the throat and hold on with all your strength as you honor God's ways. If you do this, Scripture tells us that God will bless your efforts. Thank God right now for the blessing of being a man and the opportunities that are before you, then commit yourself to making the most of those opportunities.

PRAYER

God, the veil is lifted from my eyes. I see myself the way you see me, as a man who has great competency and the aptitude to take hold of possibilities. I want to use my strength to serve those who come across my path. I see an opportunity before me of________________________ . I'm going to be a man and honor your ways as I make that happen. Amen.

GET MOVING

1. Tell God what aspects of being a man you are thankful for.
2. What is your "strength"? Can you deadlift half a ton? Do you have a sharp mind? Do you have endurance?
3. Ask two other people what your strengths are.

A MAN'S MIND

As he thinketh in his heart, so is he.

- PROVERBS 23:7 (KJV)

THE MOST POWERFUL TOOLS US MEN HAVE AT OUR disposal are our minds. Our most potent organ isn't between our legs, it is between our ears. Our minds controls our lives. Therefore, the way to take control of your life and yank it up to the next level is by taking control of your mind and the thoughts you allow yourself to think. If you think this devotional is going to suck just like all the other ones, then it is going to suck just like all the other ones. If you think you are going to get divorced just like every other male in your family, then you will eventually get divorced. If you think that you will never get out of credit card debt, then you will never get out of credit card debt.

On the other hand, thinking that you are going to meet God through the thoughts in these pages will facilitate that very thing happening. Thinking that your marriage will last will lead you to putting energy into building rather than just surviving your marriage. Believing that your current debt levels will someday be eliminated is a prerequisite to changing your financial behavior and balance sheet.

Proverbs isn't talking about deluding ourselves with happy thoughts that will mystically bring a happy life. It is telling us that our mind/body connection is real. Only we can control our minds. No one else. We are not victims, because in controlling what we think, we can control our lives. Children whine and act like victims. You are not a child. You are a man with a potent mind that can help bring things into reality.

PRAYER

God, thank you for the mind you have given me and the power to control it. Today I commit to giving more of my mind space to you because I want more of your power. Amen.

GET MOVING

1. What area of your life or mind feels out of control?
2. Today, take one unusual step of self-control by making a choice to refrain from doing something. Example: If your anger is out of control, refuse to post a response on social media.

DAY 06

YOU ARE HIS SON

For you did not receive the spirit of slavery to fall back into fear, but you have received the Spirit of adoption as sons, by whom we cry, "Abba! Father!" The Spirit himself bears witness with our spirit that we are children of God, and if children, then heirs—heirs of God and fellow heirs with Christ, provided we suffer with him in order that we may also be glorified with him.

- ROMANS 8:15-17

ABBA ISN'T JUST THE NAME OF A SWEDISH BAND from the '70s. It is also an ancient word that means "Daddy." That is a word I don't remember ever calling my dad. I was adopted as an infant, and as great as my family was, I always felt something was off. Was it because we weren't an emotionally expressive family, or was it because I had been separated from my own biological parents at birth? Though I don't know the cause, I now know what I was feeling. Despite the fact that I had been adopted, I was still living like an orphan, and I suspect many of you continue to do the same thing today, long after leaving your parents' houses.

The orphan mindset is one of emotional, intellectual, and spiritual slavery. We don't feel free to enjoy life even when we are doing well. We become a slave to our perceived reality. Orphans:

- Don't think anyone or anything else is there to backstop them.
- Are protective of their stuff because there is only so much porridge to go around.
- Are jealous of and/or bitter toward those who have more.
- Believe that the only source of provision in our life is our own efforts.

Orphans often build a successful American life with many accomplishments and digits in their bank account; but what is lacking is a joy-filled relationship with God. The kind of relationship that recognizes the blessings He's given to us. The kind of relationship which makes us feel secure and reminds us that there is an inheritance coming our way in the future—one we haven't had to earn.

Do you want to break the orphan mindset and the enslavement it brings? If you have been adopted into God's family, you are His son. YOU are His son. You can be so close to Him that you call Him "Daddy" while resting in the strength He has to cover your back and bring blessings you haven't worked for.

If you feel far from God, maybe it is because you are not yet in His family. This isn't discouraging but rather encouraging because there is a solution to your sense of disconnectedness. You can be adopted right now. Do you want to be in the family of God? Do you want His covering and protection? Do you want to abide by the family's standards? Well then tell Him "yes" right now! Make this your prayer . . .

PRAYER

(IF YOU WANT TO JOIN GOD'S FAMILY FOR THE FIRST TIME)

God, I want to be in your family. As I receive Jesus into my life, please receive me into your family. I want to be a content and productive family member for the rest of my life. This is my vow. Amen.

PRAYER

(IF YOU HAVE ALREADY JOINED GOD'S FAMILY BUT WANT A CLOSER CONNECTION TO HIM)

Dad, I want to feel more of a connection with you. I open myself up to the reality that I'm still here and doing as well as I am because you have been a good Dad to me. I'm sorry for thinking so little of your ability to take care of me. I want to go a different direction today, with a different mindset. I'm turning away from my inner orphan and kicking that butthead out of my life. You are a good Dad. Amen.

GET MOVING

1. What's one area in which you tend to feel or react like an orphan?
2. Decide right now on a different action you will take in that area. For example, if you tend to feel jealous or bitter toward a successful co-worker, look for ways to encourage and bless them.
3. If you prayed the prayer to join God's family

for the first time, tell someone (perhaps the person who got you this book). This is a time to celebrate!

DAY 07

YOU HAVE AN ENEMY

The thief comes only to steal and kill and destroy. I came that they may have life and have it abundantly.

- JOHN 10:10

NO LIFE EVER SUCKS BY RANDOM CHANCE. DO WE think it is an accident that things go wrong in our lives? Sometimes, things go wrong because we go wrong. When we shoot ourselves in the foot, we can't blame a spiritual entity. At the same time, there is an enemy who wants something from you, and his name is Satan. He wants your faith. He wants it to shrivel and die. He wants to destroy your relationship with God. He came to Adam and Eve in the very beginning because he was trying to spoil what God had created.

Satan will do whatever he can to steal the joy of being aligned with God. He will tempt one person with gobs of money and another with practices that will lead to bankruptcy. He will push one person to achieve a perfect body and infect another with cancer. He will lead one man to idolize his all-American family and push another to relational frustration. Some who have it all are deluded by their success and don't believe they need God. Others who have nothing are distracted by their physical needs and reject God because they perceive that He has not done enough for them. In both cases, they have been stolen from. When people turn from God, the thief has won.

It helps me to fight off doubts, fears, and problems when I realize I'm in the ring with an identifiable entity who wants to take me down. It gets personal. Today I hope it gets personal for you. The Enemy has come to take away your life—to squash your joy and bring complication and heartache.

Alternatively, Jesus has come to give you life and to give it in abundant measures. It isn't an accident when things go wrong, and it isn't an accident when things go right. Jesus is here with you, right now, just waiting for you to let Him get in the ring with you.

Something may happen today that will remind you that you are in a struggle. It is in the struggle that we lean into Jesus who is our champion. In Him we can have abundant life. Take it personal when you get hit in the mouth by the Enemy and realize you are not alone.

PRAYER

God, today I will not cower in fear. While things may be exploding around me, I trust in your protection as I do what needs to be done. I thank you that my difficulties are light and momentary compared to starvation and execution happening around the world to other men who have faith in you. Give me life abundantly. Amen.

GET MOVING

1. Stand tall and strong and say out loud, "God, you have made me a warrior who will endure."
2. Identify where you are lacking and ask God to abundantly give to you in those areas.

DAY 08

RESISTING THE ENEMY

Be sober-minded; be watchful. Your adversary the devil prowls around like a roaring lion, seeking someone to devour. Resist him, firm in your faith, knowing that the same kinds of suffering are being experienced by your brotherhood throughout the world.

- 1 PETER 5:8-9

THE FIRST TIME I WAS IN SOUTH AFRICA, I STAYED in a game reserve. One night, I was awoken by what sounded like loud and obnoxious groaning. When the sound grew louder and louder, I went outside, drawn by curiosity to explore.

On the other side of a gravel access road, wedged between two ten-foot chain link fences, sat a male lion, yawning. All of a sudden, a maintenance vehicle came down the road, and this previously docile animal turned into 450 pounds of moving terror. The speed and agility of this beast was awe-inspiring as he chased the truck along the fence line like a Jack Russell in your neighbor's yard would chase a car.

We often talk about how Jesus is known as "The Lion of Judah," which makes me stand in awe of Him. But Scripture calls the devil a "roaring lion" as well. The evil one isn't as powerful as the Lion of Judah, but he is loud and obnoxious. He wants to devour you. He is prowling up and down the fence line of your life trying to find an opening to dart through. Sometimes he gets in because we leave the gate open, and sometimes because he climbs the fence.

We have an enemy who isn't trying to just bring more tension to our lives, but who is actually trying to destroy our lives. Our response is to "resist." We can't kill the Enemy, but we can resist his temptations which are roaring in our lives. You know exactly where you are tempted. You know exactly how he is trying to devour you. You don't have to be a victim. Your life is your responsibility. You have the power to resist. Don't live in fear; live with the awareness that someone is against you but you can do something about it.

Don't be fearful but be sober-minded and watchful. Life is a battle.

PRAYER

Father, I'm not fearful of the Enemy, but indignant. He has no right to scream in my face and cause me to doubt you. I'm not a victim and I refuse to act as one. Give me strength today to resist. Amen.

GET MOVING

1. Identify where you hear the most roaring and ask God to forgive you for when you haven't resisted.
2. You don't have to only hear roaring; you can roar yourself. Take on an aggressive posture like you would if you were about to be attacked in an alley and defiantly roar that you will not shrink from following your God.

DAY 09

FORSAKING THE SMALL THINGS OF CHILDREN

When I was a child, I spoke like a child, I thought like a child, I reasoned like a child. When I became a man, I gave up childish ways.
- 1 CORINTHIANS 13:11

IN SOME WAYS, I'M LIKE A CHILD. I LIKE TO PLAY. I enjoy detaching from the real world. My humor has been frozen at the junior high level. God loves children and He encourages us to be like them in some ways. Child-like faith is something we should all aspire to.

But a child doesn't have perspective. A child isn't working toward a larger and longer-term vision. A child doesn't see that there are aspects of his character that are unacceptable and will at least limit his potential and at worst lead to his destruction. This destruction follows him as he grows. A man may not be sure exactly when it was he left childhood, but he and everyone around him knows he isn't a child anymore.

Most people know they don't want to be a child, but they haven't shaken adolescence from their lifestyle. These days, twenty-five-year-olds still live with their parents and are trying to "find themselves," and forty-five-year-olds keep wishing for a life void of commitment and sacrifice. In ancient cultures, when males could have an erection and ejaculate, they were expected to do manly things like defend their clan, add economic value to their society, and start a family. Don't be a child. Be a man. Welcome the complexity and difficulty of a life that has adult problems. Adult problems mean we are operating as men in the nitty-gritty of life. Rise above your big wheel and lollipops. Live like a full-grown, mentally-vibrant, spiritually-deep man.

PRAYER

God, I don't want the life I used to have. I want to learn to love the life I'm building right now. You aren't just my God. You are my Heavenly Father. I need your help growing out of ________________________ . I welcome your presence which seeks to advance and not slow down my development. Amen.

GET MOVING

1. In what area of your life are you still thinking or acting like a child?
2. Today, take one step to eradicate that childishness. For example, if you're stuck in a dead-end job, take some time today and actually write down the plan it will take to get you to a new place. Don't just think about it, write it down and make it concrete.

DAY 10

YOUR PRESENT PURPOSE

The Lord will fulfill his purpose for me; your steadfast love, O Lord, endures forever. Do not forsake the work of your hands.

- PSALM 138:8

ONE OF THE GREATEST SELLING BOOKS, OUTSIDE THE Bible, has been Rick Warren's *The Purpose Driven Life*. The reason this book is attractive to so many is that people are desperate to know that they're doing something that truly matters. But real purpose is not something we can figure out on our own, as if we were the authors of our own purposes. God is the author of the purpose for your life. He has made your life possible and has given you unique gifts and opportunities. Since He has made you and is doing something in you, you simply need to look around at what is before you.

There are a rare few who have the purpose of

preaching to millions as Billy Graham did or revolutionizing our technological devices like Steve Jobs did. For most of us, our purposes are more yeomanlike but just as important. If you have fathered a child, your purpose is to raise that life to exceed yours through pursuing a relationship of love and discipline with them. If you have a relationship with Jesus, your purpose is to abide in His presence on a daily basis. If you have a neighbor, your purpose is to love your neighbor as yourself.

I have a child, a relationship with Jesus, and a few neighbors. I also have a church I started which needs to be led well. I have a purpose to bring more people into our church and to deepen the faith of those who are already a part of it. Recently I've come to understand that God has a purpose for me to help people across the nation with spiritual concepts in an "everyman" voice, which is why this devotional exists in the first place.

What are the absolutes that God has already placed in your life? Put your head down, get after them, and stop looking to the left and right for what might possibly could be. Plow horses wear blinders because they don't need to be concerned about the crops in fields around them. They have their purpose straight ahead of them. It is the straight line of broken earth that enables a seed to bring forth fruit. Put your own blinders on and plow the field where God put you. In doing so, you will experience the faithfulness of God that will yield more accomplishments than you could ever accomplish on your own.

PRAYER

Father, thank you for planting me where I am with opportunities and responsibilities. I'm sorry for not being satisfied with where I am and dreaming of a distant pasture that may be better. I'm not where I am or who I am by accident. You won't forsake me because your love won't allow it. Amen.

GET MOVING

1. Pull out your calendar and look at your day. What's one purpose that God has put in front of you today?
2. Take the next five minutes to sit, listen for God, and decide how He wants you to "plow that field" today. Then go and do it.

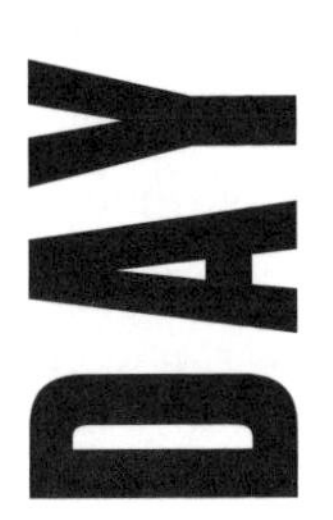

SUCCESS THROUGH COUNSEL

Without counsel plans fail, but with many advisers they succeed.

- PROVERBS 15:22

THERE IS NOTHING GREAT IN MY LIFE THAT HAS BEEN accomplished with only my own energy. God has brought advisers to me who have helped me escape danger and scale mountain tops. Our own mental and spiritual resources aren't enough to build a great life. Every great business has had investors who brought capital to the table. Likewise, we need the wisdom capital of others if we are to be successful messengers of God's good news.

Do you want success? A key ingredient is having a personal board of advisers. Not the kind that satisfy the corporate structural requirements of the IRS. God wants us to have a band of brothers who can speak into the important places of our life. We aren't smart enough to make all of our decisions on our own. We need the power of other minds speaking into our mind.

I don't make a major spending decision without the counsel of a brother. I won't take on a new job responsibility without gaining insight from a qualified, mature friend. This devotional came as a result of the counsel of advisers who told me I had something to offer and should expend energy to try to help others who might need it.

You probably have qualified people around you who you could ask into your life. It is as simple as asking someone you respect, "Would you mind giving me some advice about my profession?" Or, "Would you mind hearing me out about a difficulty I'm having in a relationship?" Inviting wise people into our lives to speak to our blind spots is a surefire way to protect ourselves from sinful or foolish missteps and to strengthen the bond with someone who may become a genuine brother.

PRAYER

God, help me to notice the gifts you have placed into my life in the form of other men with sound minds. Right now, there is a person I am thinking of, and I commit to open a conversation with him which could result in a more powerful, potent, and thriving life. Amen.

GET MOVING

1. Make a list of the three people most qualified to be your board of advisers. If you are having trouble thinking of people you can trust, then start thinking about how to build more meaningful friendships.
2. Call one or all of those people and say to them, "I've been thinking about you and how fortunate I am to have you in my life. Would you be okay if I called you from time to time to get some counsel on key decisions?"

DAY 12

THE LOST ART OF FRIENDSHIP

A man of many companions may come to ruin, but there is a friend who sticks closer than a brother.

- PROVERBS 18:24

WHEN WE ARE YOUNGER, FRIENDSHIPS SEEM TO JUST happen. As a youngster, my friends were those who lived down the street. We bonded over building treehouses and playing pickup football games. In high school, I made friends through formal sports, building relationships with the guys on my team. In college, it was the guys I roomed with. For some reason, as we age, it becomes harder to develop and maintain friendships, but these relationships are actually more important than ever.

God Himself lives in community as a triune God: Father, Son, and Holy Spirit. King David likewise had strong friendships with the prophet Nathan, Jonathan, and his "mighty men" as he made his march to greatness. Jesus' twelve disciples weren't just underlings but actual life-giving friends who walked with Him for the whole of His ministry on earth.

We don't have many models for friendships like these in the modern world because we live in a time of acquaintances. Acquaintances are easy to come by. They are the ones we meet at work but never keep up with after a job change. Acquaintances are our next-door neighbors who we wave to but know very little about. But what about a friend who sticks closer than a brother? Do you have someone you could call to cover your mortgage for a month? Do you have someone you could confess an extramarital affair to? Do you have someone you would take a fun vacation with?

If there is one discipline I could magically bestow on you, it wouldn't be the ability to read and comprehend the Bible daily. It wouldn't be the yearning to spend time every day on your knees in prayer. It would be the ability to choose and develop the right friendships. The brothers close to us will bring us laughter, wisdom, support, and meaning.

We have to go back to the deep friendships of our childhoods. We may not have the pastimes we once had, and it's doubtful that any of us will be building treehouses together anytime soon. But we have new things to build: honest relationships, bonds of accountability, commitments to encourage and occasionally admonish one another. If Jesus Himself needed brothers to live life with, then we do too, and what a blessing it is to live like Jesus in that way.

PRAYER

God, I feel lonely. Please bring men into my life whom I can develop friendships with. I also want to thank you for my friendship(s) with ____________________ . Please bless them as they have blessed me. Life is too important to live it alone. Amen.

GET MOVING

1. Text a friend or a potential friend a simple message that says, "I was just thinking of you. I hope all is well with you. I appreciate you for ______________."
2. If you are friend-starved, identify a way to get around other men to have some fun, whether that means joining a Bible study or an intra-

mural sports team. This is a key starting point for friendship.

DAY 13

THE POWER OF A YOUNG MAN

Let no one despise you for your youth, but set the believers an example in speech, in conduct, in love, in faith, in purity.

- 1 TIMOTHY 4:12

GO TO ANY BIG NCAA SPORTING EVENT AND YOU will eventually see the wave go through the stands. Where does the wave originate? From the student section. Why? Because young people are full of energy. They're initiators—the kinds of people who get things started and get things done. Scripture is filled with examples of young people chosen by God to accomplish His will. David and Daniel were both young men when God called them. Arguably the greatest woman in the history of the world was Jesus' mother, Mary, and scholars are united in that she was a young teenager when she became pregnant with our Savior.

Jesus, too, was very intentional in including the

idealistic energy of young men and women in His movement, though you might not know this from the movies. Every production on the life of Jesus depicts His disciples as middle-aged men. Wrong. All the disciples other than Peter were teenagers. How do we know that? Jesus paid the temple tax through a miracle and only He and Peter needed to pay: everyone else was under nineteen (Matthew 17:24-27).

While our culture is youth-obsessed, it is also increasingly historically clueless. Every older World War II movie shows soldiers in their thirties. Wrong. The vast majority of soldiers were under twenty-one. They were flying planes as "fly boys," maneuvering huge tanks, and becoming the greatest army the world has ever known.

Paul's disciple Timothy was also young. We don't know how young, but he was clearly youthful enough for it to be a problem for some people—so much so that Paul wrote today's key verse as an encouragement and a reminder that God can work through young people. Let this verse encourage you too: if you are young, you are important. Don't be upset about the opportunities that aren't available to you right now. Many people who are older than you would trade places in a minute in order to have your health and energy. To go back in time to when we had fewer scars is a positive proposition.

Over twenty years ago, I answered an ad in the back of a magazine from a group of thirty-somethings who were trying to find a pastor to start a church to reach their friends. My wife, Lib, and I left our hometown, our extended family, lifelong friendships, and a comfortable job backed by a stable denomination. What we were offered in return was a salary of 40K for one year. At the end of that time we would fail or go to the next level. Our ability to make this move was easier for me to make at thirty than it would have been at fifty. It required untold sacrifice for years, but it also set me up for untold blessings. I'm so glad I made that move and didn't let my doubts, youth, or lack of experience get in my way.

Grab your life by the throat and live it. This is the time for you to make aggressive moves and to explore the life your God has for you.

PRAYER

Lord, you are so good and generous. Thank you for bringing me as far as you have and giving me increased energy and opportu-

nities to serve you as I age. I commit to have that attitude today. Amen.

GET MOVING

1. List the positives of being your age and thank God for the season you are in.
2. Look for someone older with whom you want to spend more time. If you already have an idea of who that might be, reach out to them right now and ask for some of their time. Set a date and time and stick to it.

DAY 14

THE POWER OF AN AGING MAN

When Methuselah had lived 187 years, he fathered Lamech. Methuselah lived after he fathered Lamech 782 years and had other sons and daughters. Thus all the days of Methuselah were 969 years, and he died. When Lamech had lived 182 years, he fathered a son and called his name Noah, saying, "Out of the ground that the LORD has cursed, this one shall bring us relief from our work and from the painful toil of our hands." Lamech lived after he fathered Noah 595 years and had other sons and daughters. Thus all the days of Lamech were 777 years, and he died. After Noah was 500 years old, Noah fathered Shem, Ham, and Japheth.

- GENESIS 5:25-32

SCRIPTURE THAT CONTAINS A LOT OF NAMES AND numbers is rarely inspiring to me. I mean, 969 years old—can you imagine? We don't know exactly why as the Bible progresses lifespans decrease, but I do know that today's environment is very hostile to old age. Not just because of pollution and other environmental effects; it is emotionally hostile to the very concept of aging. Noah's best and most productive days were ahead of him at 500, yet our culture believes that once you turn fifty you are nearly irrelevant.

Aging shouldn't be an emotionally stressful thing. Rather, it is a spiritually invigorating thing because a life well lived qualifies you for more opportunities for the rest of life. Instead of my life winding down at fifty-three, I feel it is winding up! I feel prepped to be a spiritual father figure to a lot of people outside my church community at the same time that I'm more equipped to draw people into that community. I'm drawn to increase and widen my awareness rather than narrow it.

Many people doubt the numbers that are in the Bible. But the truth that the Bible hammers again and again is that the older we are, the more potency we have. Noah was 600 when he got a vision to build an ark. Ray Kroc didn't start McDonald's until he was fifty. Clint Eastwood's directing career didn't begin until he qualified for social security, and he made his last film—possibly his best—at age eighty-eight.

While the younger generations have anxiety in epic proportions, the older generations are stricken with epic lethargy. Noah shows us that this lethargy is self-imposed. If you are older, chop-chop. Keep going and keep your eyes open for a new thing. You are uniquely prepared for things today that you weren't when you were young. Don't buy the lie that youth alone is to be exalted. Be like Noah and begin building your own ark today.

PRAYER

Lord, you are so good and so patient. Thank you for bringing me as far as you have and giving me increased opportunities to serve you as I age. Lord, help me to serve you faithfully today so that my tomorrow will have even more possibilities of serving you. I commit to have that attitude today. Amen.

GET MOVING

1. Imagine for a moment that you know for sure that you will live to be 200. No matter how old you are now, you wouldn't even be half-

way through. If that were true, how would you approach the preparation and opportunities of today differently? Would your stress level change?

2. Pick one change of perspective from that 200-year outlook and live it out today.

DAY 15

SUPERHUMAN POWER

And they were all filled with the Holy Spirit and began to speak in other tongues as the Spirit gave them utterance . . . And at this sound the multitude came together, and they were bewildered, because each one was hearing them speak in his own language. And they were amazed and astonished . . . But others mocking said, "They are filled with new wine." But Peter, standing with the eleven, lifted up his voice and addressed them: "Men of Judea and all who dwell in Jerusalem, let this be known to you, and give ear to my words. For these people are not drunk, as you suppose, since it is only the third hour of the day."

- ACTS 2:4-15

GOD EXISTS AS ONE GOD IN A TRINITY OF THREE PERSONS: Father, Son, and Holy Spirit. The Holy Spirit doesn't dwell in a building, but in the bodies of people who have received Jesus. The first time God filled people is described in the scripture above. The Spirit isn't a "force" or an "aura." He is a person with the personal pronoun "He." When He inhabits your life, you have a power you didn't have before.

The first time He inhabits people in Scripture, they simultaneously utter a cacophony of sounds as they are speaking in languages they have never formally learned. This miracle was to prepare them for sharing truth with people with whom they couldn't previously communicate. It must have sounded like a beer fest. The Bible even says that onlookers thought they were drunk, and I love Peter's defense. He could have said, "These people aren't drunk because everyone knows we don't drink." But no. He says, "It is only 9:00 a.m. We don't start heavy drinking that early."

Even in this most sacred moment, Peter doesn't shy away from the realities of the world around him. This earthiness of the early church is so attractive to me. While there are all kinds of countercultural things they believe and do, they remain relatable, just as Peter does in this moment. When the power of the Holy Spirit is mixed with earthy authenticity, you get a potent cocktail with the potential for great impact. All of us would do well to replicate this combination we see in the early church. It was a potency that led to things like people coming to Christ, physical healings, spiritual exorcisms, encouragement of the masses, and a purpose that was constantly advancing.

We need more of us who have the Holy Spirit and are regularly asking Him to freshly fill us with His presence and power. We need more people ready to pair this presence and power with our authentic selves—with who we are, where we fit, and the interests God has given us. We have too many stresses and important assignments to operate only on our strength. God knows this and has provided us with a superpower. Receive it and use it.

PRAYER

Lord, I want everything you have to give me. Would you fill me right now with a fresh filling of the Spirit? I want Him to live in me, and I want to live a life marked with your power. Please pour your presence into my life in a fresh way. Amen.

GET MOVING

1. Do you know anyone who is definitely filled with the Holy Spirit? Ask them if they will

put their hands on you and pray for you. Frequently in the Bible this has led to more power.

2. Is there anything in your life that the Holy Spirit wouldn't like? Work to eliminate that today. In doing so, you are saying to Him, "I want to be the kind of environment that you are comfortable living in."

DAY 16

WEAKER VESSELS

Likewise, husbands, live with your wives in an understanding way, showing honor to the woman as the weaker vessel, since they are heirs with you of the grace of life, so that your prayers may not be hindered.

- 1 PETER 3:7

THIS IS ONE OF THOSE VERSES I DON'T KNOW HOW TO perfectly interpret. How is a wife a "weaker vessel?" I know wives who can do more pushups than their husbands. I know men who are much weaker than their wives emotionally. Bearing a child is to strongly endure terrible pain, while many men whine about a tiny bee sting. Too many people look for reasons to doubt the Bible and this verse will help you if that is your goal.

But if your goal is to have a life that works—a life of power, a life where your relationships are healthy, a life where you have prayers that are being answered with a healthy dosage of "yes"—then just do what God says. If I treat my wife like she is a priceless vase from the Ming Dynasty, then she feels valued and our marriage wins. When I treat her the way God tells me to treat her, then He is valued and there is less blockage in our relationship, which leads to my prayers not being hindered by a skeptical spirit.

Real life example: Most mornings, I'm the first in my house to wake up. I've recently made it my goal to take my wife coffee every morning while she is still in bed. Is she "strong" enough to get up and get her own coffee? Obviously. But I do this because this simple action communicates value to my wife. It makes her feel seen, loved, and appreciated. It's not about me showing my strength, but about showing my wife, through my actions, that she is important to me.

Instead of wrestling over the phrase "weaker vessel," I'd challenge you to take this verse by faith and just do it. There are enough cynics in the world who need proof for everything. Be a man who operates on a different level in honoring the wishes of God even when you don't understand them. When we do this, we are more likely to see God say "yes" to more of our prayers.

Trusting what the Bible says regarding how to treat your wife and experiencing blessings on the other side is a discipline you can use again and again.

Trust what the Bible says about the need to pray for your enemy. Trust what the Bible has to say about generosity. Trust what the Bible has to say about sex. God isn't interested in us agreeing with Him, He is interested in us obeying Him. When we do, we are the ones who win.

PRAYER

Lord, I'm sorry for being cynical and always looking for an out. I commit this day to honor the women in my life with a strong tenderness which gives them confidence and security. I also thank you for the woman you have given me in marriage or may someday give me in marriage. Push me to be the kind of man that she is thankful for. Amen.

GET MOVING

1. Do something for a special woman in your life that communicates her value and honor.
2. Pray blessings over all the women in your life. Be specific as you talk to God.

TAKING A BULLET

Now as the church submits to Christ, so also wives should submit in everything to their husbands. Husbands, love your wives, as Christ loved the church and gave himself up for her.

- EPHESIANS 5:24-25

I KNOW GUYS WHO QUOTE THE FIRST PART OF THIS verse to their wives but aren't living the second part. Let's let the ladies figure out what applies to them while we figure out what applies to us. Their part may be difficult, but our part is death.

Love is a difficult concept for me to feel, let alone describe. As I hear some people describe what they feel when "love is in the air," I'm left feeling confused. When others gush, I listen. When others tear up, I stare forward. When others weep, I sniffle. I wish I was more emotive; it might give me another angle in understanding love.

That being said, there is very little in the written record regarding Jesus' emotions. There is also nothing that tells us how Jesus "feels" about believers who band together to become His Church. Our verse for the day says that He "loved the church," but the description is one of physical engagement not emotional feelings. He loved us by going to a cross. He could have talked His way out of it but He gave Himself up.

Lib has the hard task of being married to me. I communicate for a living, so I'll make my points powerfully and win the argument nearly every time. I can win the argument but also lose in love. She will be hurt, and our relationship will suffer.

Every husband I know would take a bullet for his wife. Every man I know secretly dreams of dying in a dramatic way that shows him to be a courageous protector of the ones he loves. The truth is you probably don't know anyone who has ever died that way. We should stop having fantasies that are conjured up by Hollywood. How about we start with making the bed? How about we not try to talk our wives into taking the vacation that we want? How about we replace the bag after we take the garbage out? How about we let our wives win the next argument?

We are only asked to love the way God has loved us. He has loved us so much that He suffered the most painful death mankind has ever invented. Crucifixion is where the word "excruciating" comes from. His love was bearing pain and sacrificing His life for you and me. If you're married, you're called to do the same for your wife.

PRAYER

Lord, I'm in awe of your love for me. I don't fully understand it but I'm also glad I'll never have to fully replicate it. I want my wife to better understand your love as I follow your example in our relationship. Please put a special blessing on her life today. I'm committed to be that blessing. Amen.

GET MOVING

1. What is a simple thing your wife loves that you can bless her with? Receiving flowers? Do that for her today.
2. For the rest of the week, do nothing to win an argument or disagreement. Lay down your

life and allow your wife to be right or have her way in every situation. Even if she is clearly in the wrong, it will be good for you to lay down your will, preferences, and life.

DAY 18

OUR GOD IS OVER IT

Therefore, if anyone is in Christ, he is a new creation. The old has passed away; behold, the new has come.

- 2 CORINTHIANS 5:17

OUR WORLD KNOWS INCREASINGLY LITTLE ABOUT grace and second chances. We believe: once a racist, always a racist; once a sex offender, always a sex offender. The world judges us by our past actions because it can't believe that anyone can truly change. I'm so thankful our God operates by a different standard.

I'm thankful that God doesn't hold my alcohol abuse in high school against me. Nor the vandalism. Nor the lies I told about girls. I'm thankful that God isn't still upset over my poor financial management as a younger man. I'm thankful God is over the last time I watched porn, which is more recent than I care to admit. He is over these things because He has made me new.

I've counseled many men who are trying to put the pieces back together after their adulterous affairs. They feel an understandable amount of shame and unworthiness. They sometimes articulate that they wish their wives would have an affair so that the playing field could be leveled. They can't imagine a world where their wives could forgive them, especially when the weight of wrongs is so unbalanced.

Initially, these feelings are understandable—necessary, even. Being distraught is a healthy part of grieving over our sin before pursuing further sanctification. But there comes a time where we have to receive forgiveness and move on. I've heard women say to their husbands, "I don't judge you any longer for your adultery. I'm over it. Let's move on." Whether you have committed a similar sin, and whether you have heard the people you've wronged say that or not, understand that God is over it, and He is moving on. He doesn't rehash all things old: He makes all things new.

Father, I'm so thankful that you look forward and not backward.

I have a lot of things in my rearview mirror which shouldn't have happened. I appreciate that my mistakes and sins haven't been in the front of your mind since the day I asked forgiveness. I can't wait to see what new things you bring me today. Amen.

GET MOVING

1. What's something in your past that you haven't moved on from?
2. Knowing what you know now, identify one thing that you would do differently from the first question (a choice, a relationship, an emotional reaction, etc.). You have now learned from your past and you are new before God. Move on and do things differently next time.

DAY 19

WHAT DO WE EXPECT FROM GOD?

Now the Lord is the Spirit, and where the Spirit of the Lord is, there is freedom.

- 2 CORINTHIANS 3:17

COMPLETE THIS SENTENCE WITH WHAT MAKES SENSE to you: "Where the Spirit of the Lord is, there is _______________." Morality . . . Reprimand . . . Coaching . . . What is your answer? Maybe it is "worship" or "deep teaching" or "feeding the poor?"

Our answer to this question tells us a lot about what we expect from God. If God were to visit you in a tangible way in the room you are in right now, what would He bring with Him? According to 2 Corinthians 3:17, He would bring freedom.

Why do we think God is primarily a puritan preacher who comes to bring morality? Or an ornery junior high teacher who comes to bring rules and a paddle? When God's Spirit is present there is an increase of life and mobility. He actually increases our capacities. He doesn't give us freedom to break His commands, but He does give us freedom to do what we couldn't do were He not a part of our lives.

Sometimes we have difficult things in our day because Jesus had difficult things in His day. None of us are immune to feeling restriction and even pain due to the season of life that we are in. That being said, I know many people who assume that if life isn't hard then they must be disappointing God. The expectation is that the closer I get to God, the more difficult my life should be.

No, the closer we get to God, the more freedom we feel. His Spirit will give you freedom that other people can't understand. Freedom to say "no" when everyone else is saying "yes." Freedom to have had your last drink of the night when other people can't say no to their sixth. Freedom to marry a good woman you choose instead of feeling the bondage of finding the elusive soulmate.

Today you can decide to live how you want to live. You have the power to live the way God wants you to live. If you don't think you do, I encourage you to ask for God's Spirit to fill you.

PRAYER

Holy Spirit fill me with a fresh portion of your presence. I want more than I have right now. I want more freedom, more power, more capacity. For this to happen, I need more of you. Take my balloon heart which is barely filled and blow it up full of your presence. Amen.

GET MOVING

1. What are you free from today that you weren't earlier? Thank God for your progress. Remind yourself of your status and write "Free" somewhere on your body.
2. If God magically freed you from something, what would it be? Today, live out that freedom in a practical way. For example, if you feel bound by an expectation to perform, find something you can cancel, and go spend time doing something freeing.

DAY 20

PRAYING FOR WHAT WE WANT

Until now you have asked nothing in my name. Ask, and you will receive, that your joy may be full.

- JOHN 16:24

PRAYER IS THE GATEWAY TO BIG THINGS. THINGS which go beyond the standard "heal my grandmother" prayers. Or "bless this food." And don't forget the classic, "Now I lay me down to sleep . . ." Prayer is the thing that must happen before and during everything that is beyond our normal human capacities.

I used to speak against praying only when we want something from God. But now I see too few people asking God for anything. I'm not sure if we are lazy, or we don't know the things He can do for us. Or maybe we believe we are so self-sufficient that it doesn't cross our mind to ask for anything.

Have you ever asked God for literal, physical healing? I always thought that was a ridiculous miracle to pray for. Well, I was right and wrong. It is a miracle, but it isn't ridiculous. Prayers I've prayed for people have led to the birth of babies, the healing of an eye disease, the healing of nerve damage in an arm, and more.

What is the last thing you voluntarily said "yes" to that you weren't sure you could do? Do you have a life that is in need of God because you are living on a high level? Or is your life so small and manageable that you don't need God? We need to have enough belief that we pray for things we can't get on our own.

Jesus encourages us to ask and to do so according to His name, or in other words His character and identity. He isn't asking us to tack "In the name of Jesus" on at the end of our prayer, as if those are the magic words that lead to fulfillment. He is asking us to pray for things that are in alignment with His desires. We need to amp up our asks and we need to do it now.

PRAYER

God, I'm sorry for not thinking that you listen to my prayers. I'm also sorry that my prayers have been small. I've been hesitant to ask you for _____________________. There has been too little faith in my life. Please say "yes" to the thing I'm asking for. I think it is something Jesus would approve of. Amen.

GET MOVING

1. What keeps you from asking for "big" things from God?
2. Spend the next two minutes asking God for something big, something you want that is beyond your capability to handle on your own.

DAY 21

THE EXAMPLE OF BEING BLESSED

For I have given you an example, that you also should do just as I have done to you. Truly, truly, I say to you, a servant is not greater than his master, nor is a messenger greater than the one who sent him. If you know these things, blessed are you if you do them.

- JOHN 13:15-17

TO BE BLESSED IS TO HAVE A LIFE THAT "WORKS." Our life works when we live it the way Jesus lived His. When this occurs, good things happen regularly, and they're not just coincidences. I'm blessed because of my choices and the choices God makes to bless my life. As Jesus says, we are blessed based on what we do.

Too many people read the Bible like a textbook, thinking that gaining knowledge will lead to blessing. Too many people believe spiritual growth equates to intellectual growth. Too many people endlessly search for new things to tickle their minds. Education does not bring life growth. Education only sets us up with opportunities for life growth in the form of blessings.

Expecting a book to help you grow when you haven't acted on what you've already read is fruitless. Hoping a preacher takes you to a new level when you haven't implemented what that person said last week is flawed thinking. Moving on to a new church after being passively engaged at your old one without taking a risk to actually meet anyone or get into community will take you nowhere spiritually.

As men, we don't just think about things, we do things. The greats of the past have built buildings, invented inventions, and created civilizations. Jesus has hardwired the need to do inside of you. Experiencing the blessings of God only comes when we *do* the teachings of God. Most people in churches need no more information. What we need is to do what we have learned. This is what transformation is. Do not be deceived by our culture that increasingly only thinks and observes. Be a doer!

PRAYER

Lord, transform me from just a hearer of your word to a doer of your word. I want to experience your blessing. Please help me as I follow your instructions. Amen.

GET MOVING

1. What's one thing that you already know but haven't done?
2. Identify how you're going to do that thing today and tell one other person about your plan.

DAY 22

THE BLESSED LIFE

If you know these things, blessed are you if you do them.

- JOHN 13:17

I RECENTLY TOOK A TRIP TO NEW ZEALAND WHERE I camped for two weeks with some friends while we explored the country. That country has a crazy wide variety of topography and climates in such a relatively small landmass. It's easy to see why *The Lord of the Rings* was filmed there.

On that trip I had my first experience with a rainforest. It was totally different than I thought it would be. I expected it to be like it is when it rains in the woods while I'm trying to hunt. It wasn't like that at all. Rain in the woods comes unpredictably with big drops and leaves unpredictably.

In the rainforest, the locals have it down to an exact science. They told us the exact kilometer marker where the rain would start, and they were right. What they didn't tell us was that this would be a moisture like the "misters" at Disney World that try to cool you off in the heat of summer. Sounds amazing, right? It is. You could live in it every day, all day, and in fact, there are many benefits to doing so.

This is what it is like when we are blessed. As I've already said earlier in this book, I'm blessed because of my choices and by the goodness of God. Following Him isn't all about head knowledge. Experiencing the life-changing intersection of God in your life will begin to happen as you DO what He says, not just learn more about Him. The locals in New Zealand could tell us exactly where the rainforest would start, and I can tell you exactly where God's blessing in your life will start: when you start to move.

PRAYER

Lord, today I commit to doing whatever I know is true. I want my life to stand out from average. Please bless me as I follow your instructions. Amen.

GET MOVING

1. Get out your phone and set a timer for sixty seconds. For that minute, you're going to sit quietly and ask God to bring to mind something that He's told you to do, but that you haven't yet done.
2. Whatever He brings to mind, tell someone else, and give them permission to pester you about it mercilessly until you do it.

DAY 23

THE PATH TO GREATNESS

But whoever would be great among you must be your servant, and whoever would be first among you must be slave of all. For even the Son of Man came not to be served but to serve, and to give his life as a ransom for many.

- MARK 10:43-45

IN THE BIBLE, WE HEAR A LOT ABOUT THE DISCIPLES James and John and their father, Zebedee. These disciples were called the "Sons of Thunder," while Zebedee himself is notable for running a very large, successful fishing business. But perhaps it was their mother whose actions are most memorable. Like many strong Jewish mothers, she is driven to push for her children's advancement, and even goes so far as to attempt to secure her sons a place in heaven on Jesus' right and left hand.

The ten other disciples are a bit indignant that Jesus entertains this request. Maybe this indignation doesn't stem from their disdain for a driven mother, maybe it's because she asks for what they all wanted and hadn't yet had the courage to ask for themselves. They would all like one of those slots. Wouldn't you? The closer to Jesus, the better!

Nevertheless, most people look at this request as brazenly selfish. Not true. Jesus never criticizes anyone from the family of Zebedee for this request. Nor does He criticize the other disciples who probably internally desire those slots. Nor does He hold you in contempt for wanting the most impactful life possible, one which results in greatness.

Jesus never rebuked anyone for wanting to be great. What He did do was clarify *how* to become great: by serving others. Jesus has the greatest and most well-known name in all of human history, and He gained that position because God granted it to Him after He served by giving up His life.

God isn't against us being great. He is against the normal paths to greatness: selfishness and self-promotion. What can you do today to serve others?

Lord, I want to be great, and I want to take the path of service

that Jesus modeled for me. I'm going to look for people to serve on this day and I will put my assets on the field of play in hopes of blessing others and increasing my greatness. Amen.

GET MOVING

1. Serving others is unusual in our culture, and we typically only do it when we have something to gain. Identify someone in your life that you would have to humble yourself to serve.
2. Now, do it. Today. Do it without recognition or praise—simply because you're after the greatness of God, not men.

DAY 24

GLORY MAKES SOME MEN WEAK

Many even of the authorities believed in him, but for fear of the Pharisees they did not confess it, so that they would not be put out of the synagogue; for they loved the glory that comes from man more than the glory that comes from God.

- JOHN 12:42-43

WE ALL SEEK GLORY AND AFFIRMATION. WE NEED TO feel that our life matters and we are on the right track. That is part of being human. For some, their political affiliations give them worth and glory while for others, it is the number of followers, friends, and subscribers. Many of us are like Judas, who played the role of Jesus' disciple but, in reality, loved money more, selling Jesus out in the process. A few verses before today's scripture, Judas criticized a generous act of worship by Mary who poured expensive perfume on Jesus' feet. He cites the standard objection of "this could have gone to the poor" when in reality he didn't think Jesus was worthy of extravagant worship. He wanted to keep the money in the disciples' coffers.

I know what it means to live for the glory that others can give me. I've been doing that for much of my life and still fight it to this day. I want the things I write to be bought by a lot of people. I like the church I lead to be drawing more and more people. More can feel like winning, and winning is good. But too often I want numbers so that I get more glory for myself, which is selfish and weak. We are weak in our quest of the glory of a large bank account. We are weak when we need the affirmation of "followers" on social media. We are weak when we need the affirmation of the masses to approve of our moral choices.

Living to get glory is like playing king of the hill on a mound of sand. That glory never lasts and never fully satisfies my thirst. But when I point to the ultimate king, Jesus, who instead of trying to rule the hill, died on it, there is a glory that never fades. Glory that comes from God to those who are faithful is a fulfilling thing.

PRAYER

Lord, I promise to not climb the hill today. May you get more attention and glory as a result of how this day is lived. Amen.

GET MOVING

1. What is one way that you tend to seek glory or affirmation?
2. Find a way to "give away" your glory in that area. For example, if you find affirmation in your bank account, find a way to be generous to someone else without them knowing about it.

DAY 25

HOW TO GET STUFF DONE

Abide in me, and I in you. As the branch cannot bear fruit by itself, unless it abides in the vine, neither can you, unless you abide in me. I am the vine; you are the branches. Whoever abides in me and I in him, he it is that bears much fruit, for apart from me you can do nothing.

- JOHN 15:4-5

THIS PASSAGE ISN'T IMPLYING THAT A MAN CAN'T DO anything without Christ. Atheists do a lot of things without Christ. But without Him, we can't do anything of significance that is beyond our own power.

No branch can support a piece of fruit unless it is tied to a trunk. Likewise, I cannot do things that are eternally significant if I am not tied to Jesus. Balancing a household budget and working fifty hours a week are things an atheist can do. But bringing life to parched souls, impacting future generations, or seeing someone be healed from a prayer you prayed is possible only through the power of Jesus.

I've heard people say, "God doesn't call us to be fruitful, He calls us to be faithful." I guess they haven't gotten around to reading what Jesus actually said. If we aren't bearing fruit, then we aren't being faithful because being faithful is being close to the vine of Christ. And being close to the vine of Christ will bring true change and impact.

Just as all trees experience winter, every branch will go through seasons of barrenness. The church I lead hasn't always grown. My finances don't always improve. My friendships have sometimes been listless. Our lives can't always be up and to the right. But if our season of faithful barrenness is stretching on for long periods of time without appropriate fruit, let's stop fooling ourselves. We likely aren't operating close to Christ. We are doing our own thing on our own power and with our own religiosity, and as Scripture says, that will lead to *nothing*. But when we abide in Christ, opportunities for powerful impact are endless.

PRAYER

Jesus, I want your power which eclipses mine. Today, help me to produce something that is luscious, juicy, and satisfying. Amen.

GET MOVING

1. Identify something fruitful that you want God to do through you.
2. Spend five minutes sometime today talking (and listening) to God about how He wants that fruitful thing to happen.

DAY 26

BALANCE IS A BAD GOAL

Six days you shall work, but on the seventh day you shall rest. In plowing time and in harvest you shall rest.

- EXODUS 34:21

SIX DAYS WORKING AND ONE DAY NOT WORKING doesn't sound like "balance." Shouldn't it be four working and three resting or, better yet, three at work and four at rest? When I hear people who aspire for balance, I rarely see people truly shutting down work to rest. They will stay home or go on a vacation, but their text, email, and social media habits remain the same.

I'm so tired of hearing people *talk* about the need for balance in our lives instead of doing it. And I'm sick of people thinking that their version of balance is going to bring results. We all need to work, and we all need to rest. Some of us need to work a lot harder. Some of us need to rest a lot harder. It is in the extremes that a great life under God's care is formed.

We need to stop associating balance with 50/50—that kind of thinking never promotes movement. But if we are talking about the kind of balance that we see in a golf swing, that is a different matter. To drive the ball far, we must shift our weight in a balanced way from one side of our body to the other. The more weight you can shift in a controlled manner, the better the shot will be.

The only balance that works in a fight is when we draw our fist back and then thrust it forward. To not draw our fist back is to not have any future power. We need to balance our lives in a way that encourages movement—working and resting in the appropriate amounts so that we can be the most productive and purposeful.

To have a life that works for the long haul, we have to be extreme workers and extreme resters.

PRAYER

God, I want my life to work. I need to have the right rhythm of hard work and unadulterated rest. I'm not sure exactly what that would look like in my life. Would you please put an idea in my mind? (Be silent for one minute.) Okay, I will try that this week. Amen.

GET MOVING

1. What idea came to mind as you were praying? Open your calendar and clear the space to make it happen within the next seven days.
2. Do something today beyond the norm. Work a longer day or take a longer lunch. At the end of the day, ask yourself if it made any difference.

DAY 27

WHO IS KING?

So Pilate said to him, "You will not speak to me? Do you not know that I have authority to release you and authority to crucify you?" Jesus answered him, "You would have no authority over me at all unless it had been given you from above. Therefore he who delivered me over to you has the greater sin." From then on Pilate sought to release him, but the Jews cried out, "If you release this man, you are not Caesar's friend. Everyone who makes himself a king opposes Caesar."

- JOHN 19:10-12

THE MOB GIVES PILATE SOME WISE COUNSEL: "EVERYone who makes himself a king opposes Caesar." Jesus had just given Pilate the spiritual truth that it is God who establishes authorities. He can establish authorities because He is the ultimate authority as the King of all creation. We would do well to not make ourselves a king. We do so when we assume that the world should revolve around us.

Men seem to outpace women in our zest for ultimate power. Exhibit A is our road rage. We are afflicted with this issue more than women. Our reaction in traffic shows that we think of ourselves as king. We get angry in the car and even use hand signals as we say or think, "How dare that person cut me off?" or "I can't believe he changed lanes without using his blinker?" or "Come on, why are people driving slow in the left lane?! I have important places to be because I am an important person—certainly more important than that loser."

The deeper spiritual principle at play here is this: anyone who makes himself a king actually opposes God. I should be serving Him and His interests, not me and my interests. When we serve the one true King, His agenda goes forward with less friction, and our lives take on more peace because we just aren't wired to bear the load of God.

PRAYER

Lord, I'm thankful that you are my ultimate authority. You are a King who is worthy of my life and praise. Today I put myself under your agenda. Amen.

GET MOVING

1. Often, anger is a clue to places where we are attempting to be king. Identify a place where you are consistently angry or frustrated.
2. What's one way that you can give up kingship in that area? For example, if you're frustrated about how your spouse handles household tasks, find one and proactively do it without being asked.

DAY 28

LET'S LIGHTEN UP

Now on the first day of the week Mary Magdalene came to the tomb early, while it was still dark, and saw that the stone had been taken away from the tomb. So she ran and went to Simon Peter and the other disciple, the one whom Jesus loved, and said to them, "They have taken the Lord out of the tomb, and we do not know where they have laid him. So Peter went out with the other disciple, and they were going toward the tomb. Both of them were running together, but the other disciple outran Peter and reached the tomb first."

- JOHN 20:1-4

THIS ACCOUNT CRACKS ME UP. MARY MAGDALENE GETS to the tomb first and earliest. Then two disciples: Peter and "the one whom Jesus loved." Who would that disciple be? John. The same disciple writing the Gospel of John that we are reading. It is like John is playfully poking at Peter: "just remember Peter . . . and I'm going to make sure everyone remembers for all of history . . . I'm the one Jesus loved!" (John 13:23, John 19:26, John 21:7). Oh, and John was also a faster runner than Peter. He beat him to the tomb, and the "disciple whom Jesus loved" made sure to record that part too.

I don't think this is prideful on John's part. I think it is playful. Too many of us are too serious when it comes to God and His truth. We only read the Bible as detectives muttering under our breath "just the facts, ma'am." There are playful parts in the Bible, and God wants us to be more playful. There are facts in the Bible that are there for the implicit purpose of adding levity. We need to lighten up to notice these little gems.

Another example is when the prophet Elijah is in a competition with prophets of the false god Baal. The first one who gets his wood pile to burn wins. The false prophets are having no luck, so Elijah taunts them with what would be in today's vernacular, "maybe your God is taking a dump" (1 Kings 18:27). Junior high humor often wins with us men, and it did with Elijah as well.

Maybe fewer people are going to church these days because they are already so weighed down with the problems of life that they can't take anything heavier laid upon their shoulders. Maybe all of us would be better served in our relationship with God if we lightened up and allowed more laughter into our lives. Your Heavenly Father has created you with the capacity to laugh. Use what He has given you.

PRAYER

Father, I want to see the lighter things in life. I want to feel the lightness of laughter more often. Please forgive me for thinking you don't have a sense of humor and help me to laugh more often. Amen.

GET MOVING

1. Search "humorous" on YouTube and have some laughs.
2. Take note of all the things that happen today that people would notice and appreciate if they were lighter.

DAY 29

THE GIVER OF NAMES

But you are a chosen race, a royal priesthood, a holy nation, a people for his own possession, that you may proclaim the excellencies of him who called you out of darkness into his marvelous light.

- 1 PETER 2:9

MY FRIEND ERIC FROM MY COLLEGE DAYS CALLS ME "the giver of names." I love to give nicknames. Eric is called "Dude" because he used to say "dude" every other sentence and in a deep drawn out voice. He calls me "the giver of names" because after I get to know people, it normally isn't long before they have a nickname. I like to think that this is because I'm like Jesus in so many ways (sarcastic humor from our previous day).

Jesus gave nicknames all the time. John was truly known as "the one Jesus loved." Jesus loved all His followers, but there was something unique about His relationship with John. In fact, there is something unique about all of Jesus' relationships with His followers, past and present. I wonder what moniker I wear before Him. "The one who builds?" or, "the one who kept getting another chance?" or, "the one who was aggressive?" Or maybe, "the one who gave grace?" I would be fine with any of these monikers but only Jesus knows if they are true and honorable.

To know someone's name is to know something about their identity. Today's scripture is full of names and identities that belong to every follower of Jesus. You are "chosen." You are also a "royal priest" who God wants to use in the lives of others. These things give you the name "holy," which means you are different and set apart from normal people who live mundane lives. You are enlisted in the highest calling possible.

No matter if you are known for being fast or slow, aggressive or tentative, a builder or a reader, there's one thing our world needs more of . . . people who know who they are. Be one of those guys.

PRAYER

Lord, today I choose to follow you and build a reputation that I would be proud of for eternity. I give this day to that goal. Amen.

GET MOVING

1. Once you know who you are, decisions become clearer. Take a name tag or piece of tape and write a name you think God has for you.
2. Stick it to your chest under your shirt and live your day that way.

DAY 30

THE HEALTH OF UNHEALTHY HABITS

When the master of the feast tasted the water now become wine, and did not know where it came from . . . the master of the feast called the bridegroom and said to him, "Everyone serves the good wine first, and when people have drunk freely, then the poor wine. But you have kept the good wine until now."

- JOHN 2:9-10

A STRONG SEGMENT OF OUR POPULATION THINKS everything should pass a health test before it has a part in your life. If cheese curls don't have the right amount of vitamins, then they should be avoided. The case against alcohol becomes stronger when you add a little religion to the mix.

You don't have to drink to have a party, but we can't deny reality, and the reality is that Jesus enabled the party to continue by creating wine out of water. This was His first miracle. Some religious types will try to convince us that it wasn't actual wine, but a grape juice substance that wasn't fermented. The problem with that belief is that the wine steward said it was the best wine of the night. He knew the difference between Opus and Welch's.

The Bible gives a lot of warnings against drunkenness. We shouldn't go to the extreme of losing our faculties, but there is also a danger in the other extreme of believing all indulgences are bad and unhealthy. God isn't a god who frowns on all pleasures. What is wrong with something you are taking in moderation that isn't hurting you? Nothing. Alcohol and cheese curls, when consumed in moderation, can be very similar to caffeine. A lot of people have caffeine and it enhances their life, but some people are addicted and it negatively affects their life. I haven't had caffeine for five years. It was negatively affecting my energy late in the day, so I eliminated it. If alcohol is affecting your life negatively in the least, you need to let it go as many brave warriors have in AA.

I'm not suggesting that you need to go out and start developing vices. Rather, I want you to gain a love for life and all it offers, while at the same time being willing to hold that life loosely. We feel uncomfortable around judgmental teetotalers because they can't let go; they hold on to their lives and their moral systems so tightly that they seem ready to explode at any minute. Without a way to detach from the monotonous aspects of life—without the occasional worldly pleasure to pursue in moderation—we risk becoming unhealthy, uptight people.

Our God has created us with the healthy desire, even *need*, for pleasure. We can find that pleasure through finger painting or through two fingers of whiskey. Your Heavenly Father is more concerned about your spiritual formation than He is about your coffee habit. And He is also great with you having healthy or neutral pleasure.

PRAYER

God, help me to see what is unhealthy in my life and to eliminate or lessen it. Help me to stop putting rules in my life that you haven't clearly established. You are good to give me the freedoms I have. Thank you for not being a totalitarian entity. Amen.

GET MOVING

1. Is there anything you engage in regularly that is pure freedom or passion? Motorcycles, hik-

ing, model airplanes, homebrew, cigars, and so on all fit the bill. Identify the thing in your life that God can use to bless you with freedom and pleasure.

2. When's the last time you engaged in that activity? If the answer is more than six days ago, it's been too long. Find time to do it ASAP. If less than that, get another dose of it on your calendar soon.

DAY 31

FALSE SPIRITUALITY

Even Satan disguises himself as an angel of light. So it is no surprise if his servants, also, disguise themselves as servants of righteousness. Their end will correspond to their deeds.
- 2 CORINTHIANS 11:14-15

PASSAGES LIKE THIS ARE EYE-OPENERS. PEOPLE ARE having a lot of spiritual experiences. Next time you are having some beers with the guys and want to go beneath the veneer ask, "Has anyone had a spiritual experience you can't fully explain?" Do that with a group of guys who are willing to open up and you will be shocked by the number of stories they tell.

Today we use the word "spiritual" for anything that is good. But the truth is that there are a lot of things that are spiritual that are bad because of a bad spiritual entity. He is known as "Satan," "The Evil One," "The Devil," "The Adversary," "Lucifer," and other names. He also has a bunch of minions who are demons.

These spiritual forces are okay with you having a lot of nice things. They are fine with you receiving deeper teachings. They are also okay with you having cool experiences. They will often instigate an experience that gives you a taste of the transcendent. We think that all these experiences are from God, but not necessarily so.

Satan wants only to keep you away from the one true God and the spirituality that is under His domain. Satan will give us feel-good spiritual experiences. He may even allow us to see visions and angelic beings. Some of us have experienced the dark side and we know it. Others of us have experienced the dark side and we don't know it, because Satan disguises himself in a spirituality that is warm and attractive.

The "angel of light" is trying to dupe us all. True spirituality always has Jesus at the center and gives glory to His Heavenly Father. Be very wary of anything outside these lines.

PRAYER

Lord, I want to experience more than just the physical life I can see with my eyes and understand with my mind. But I want to experience that which is real and is of you. Grow in me a keen sense of discernment. Amen.

GET MOVING

1. The simplest way to distinguish true spirituality from false spirituality is not to study the lies, but rather to know the truth inside and out. Open up YouTube and find a magician or illusionist. Watch a few minutes of their act. Remind yourself that, even though it looks real, there's a catch. That's an appropriate visual for how Satan tries to trick us with false spirituality. It might look real, but beneath the surface, something is off.
2. Spend a few minutes reading and memorizing a Bible verse that describes God's character—something like 2 Samuel 22:32-36.

DAY 32

AMERICA: THE LAND OF THE FEARFUL

For God gave us a spirit not of fear but of power and love and self-control.

- 2 TIMOTHY 1:7

WHENEVER WE ARE AFRAID, IT'S A CLEAR INDICATION that something is wrong. God doesn't generate the kind of fear that saps joy and limits opportunities. We see this problem constantly in our country.

We call ourselves the "land of the free," but most of us feel fearful more often than we feel free. We have more anxiety in our country, more medications for anxiety, more paranoia, more neuroses, more seat belts, more helmets, more insurance policies, more disaster plans, more OSHA rules, more general stress about what could go wrong than we know what to do with.

Fear keeps us from seeking to understand people who are different from us. It keeps us from exploring new opportunities. It keeps us from feeling free to be who God has created us to be. When we receive Jesus, we receive the Holy Spirit, and that Spirit equips and empowers. He doesn't shackle and limit.

Do you want to ride a motorcycle but are afraid you'll wreck? Take a riders' safety course. Do you want to embark on a new career but are afraid you will fail? Take the leap—the worst that can happen is you have to reverse course. Do you want to ask her out but afraid she will say no? Do it anyway. Rejection is part of life. The sooner you get used to it, the more resilient you will be and the less limitations you will place on yourself.

God loves you, and He has given you power and self-control. You are not a victim. You can take control of your life because the God who has created your life has given you the Holy Spirit to sustain your life. Fear and freedom are opposites. Today, choose God's freedom and turn down the fear in your life.

PRAYER

God, I don't want to be fearful. I'm sorry for not trusting you and for constantly believing and planning for bad things that never happen. I need your spirit of power and self-control to help me crush the lie of fear. Amen.

GET MOVING

1. What are you afraid of? Ponder the first thing that came to your mind for a minute. What keeps you in that fearful state? What might God want to show you on the other side of that fear?
2. Identify a step you could take in the direction of overcoming that fear and do it today.

DAY 33

GREATER THINGS

Truly, truly, I say to you, whoever believes in me will also do the works that I do; and greater works than these will he do, because I am going to the Father.

- JOHN 14:12

JESUS GIVES US AN AUDACIOUS VISION. A VISION THAT we will be able to do greater things than what He accomplished on the earth. This is crazy but true. In the Book of Acts, we see His followers welcome thousands to the Jesus movement in one afternoon. He never did that. Since then, we have seen His followers start hospitals, orphanages, and successful businesses that have lifted people out of poverty—all things which He never did.

Often people of faith believe that if someone wants great things then they aren't content enough, or that they must be out of the will of God. If someone has aspirations, we think they just aren't happy with what God has given them. In some circles, to be a good person is to be a person without big goals. Definitely not goals that could result in you having more responsibility. Definitely not goals that could cause you to be unlike your peer group. Definitely nothing "great."

You may have a goal of getting married. Too small. Have a goal of a deep and fulfilling marriage that never ends in divorce, and of having kids who will be a blessing to you for the rest of your life.

You may have a goal of graduating college. Still too small. Have a goal of knowing that the more education you have, the more equipped and better positioned you are to impact culture.

You may have a goal of reaching the executive suite. Again, too small. Have a goal of reaching the elite in the Kingdom of God who are known for their faithfulness in going after big dreams that affect the masses for eternity.

God has not called and equipped us to have a manageable life, but rather a life of greatness—one in which you do even greater things than He did.

PRAYER

God, I'm done with thinking small. I'm done with settling for what those around me experience. I want to do and experience things that are beyond the norm. I'm going to live today with that goal in mind. Amen.

GET MOVING

1. What is one of your current "normal" goals?
2. Take five minutes and rewrite it into something audacious and God-sized. Write it down and put it somewhere where you'll see it for the next week.

DAY 34

EXPANDING OUR TERRITORY

Jabez called upon the God of Israel, saying, "Oh that you would bless me and enlarge my border, and that your hand might be with me, and that you would keep me from harm so that it might not bring me pain!" And God granted what he asked.

- 1 CHRONICLES 4:10

TWENTY YEARS AGO, A SMALL BOOK WAS WRITTEN ON Jabez and his prayer.[1] Millions of copies were sold, and many Christians went ape over the premise of the book: we should be like Jabez and pray for our territory to be expanded. The Bible refers to Jabez and his prayer as "honorable," so I say we should be praying this prayer as well.

The truth of the matter is, right now, people in our world are taking new ground—building successful businesses, getting elected to higher offices, or influencing culture through the arts. Why shouldn't those people be the men who are reading this book? Do you think God wants a dishonorable man to increase His influence or an honorable one? The fact that you are reading this right now puts you in the minority of people who want more of God and who God may want more for.

Truth be told, when your influence, wealth, reputation, and business grow, so do the responsibilities. Boys don't want responsibility. Men welcome it. It is much easier to ask God for wealth, but asking for territory means we are taking on the responsibility of pioneering and managing. Being a part of something with growing numbers means taking care of people who are taking care of those numbers. Increasing our territory isn't about showing up on a list of achievers so much as it is about taking a holistic approach to the people who are in your life.

As a younger leader I used to hate the walk to my car during my lunch break. As I walked down the steps to the parking lot, I would see all the other cars of staff members who were depending on me for their livelihood. While stressful, it was also a helpful reminder that I'm to holistically care for those who I employ. This includes not bringing them needless harm or pain while we ask the same from God.

Stop listening to people who think you shouldn't

want more. God needs honorable people who will take territory that He wants taken and who will accept the responsibility that comes along with it. Go after the dream of making your life count.

PRAYER

God, I want more. I want more of you and more of whatever you want for me. I am up for more territory. You can give me responsibility, and I'm game for any blessings you want to send my way. If you have anything going on today, I want to be a part of it. Amen.

GET MOVING

1. Where do you feel God calling you to take new ground? How can you act on that today?
2. While taking new ground, we must also maintain the territory God has already given us. Today, identify one way you can better care for the ground you already have—developing a relationship, mentoring

someone, creating a smoother process, even repairing part of your house. Go and do it.

DAY 35

A GOOD IDEA IS A GOD IDEA

For it has seemed good to the Holy Spirit and to us to lay on you no greater burden than these requirements: that you abstain from what has been sacrificed to idols, and from blood, and from what has been strangled, and from sexual immorality. If you keep yourselves from these, you will do well. Farewell.

- ACTS 15:28-29

JESUS WAS A JEW, AS WERE ALL OF HIS EARLY FOLlowers. When you are doing something alongside other people who think and act like you, it's simple. Jesus and His followers all understood their cultural heritage and appreciated the same customs and traditions. Things get more difficult when you begin inviting in those who were once considered outsiders. Early Christians expected all new followers of Jesus to fold into a worldview grounded in a Jewish way of life. But in reality, no thirty-year-old Gentile man who comes to Christ wants to be circumcised.

How the apostles deal with a sticky management situation is shocking to some but admirable to me. How do they handle tension between Jewish and Gentile believers and their preferences? They compromise. The word "compromise" is almost always negative in faith circles, and yet it is what is often necessary at critical junctures for a movement to march forward.

The apostles come to the conclusion to have the Gentile believers keep just three Jewish practices. Why these three and not others? Why not one or two? Did God speak to the Jewish leaders who made this decision? All we know is that "it seemed good" that this was the right course forward.

This is very freeing. We can make decisions of consequence without "hearing from the Lord." If it seemed like a good idea and the Holy Spirit didn't bring evidence to the contrary, then they were going to go forward. Someone once told me that a good idea isn't a God idea. Don't tell that to the leadership of the early church.

How many marriages would be better off with compromise? How many businesses would be thriving if they opened themselves up to the perspectives of others and came to compromise? As the conservative church and the LGBTQ community continue to be at war with each other, imagine what would happen if the Church worked to reach a compromise that allowed for freedom of expression while maintaining religious freedom? Be a man who is open to ideas which compromise what you would ultimately want, but also don't cause you to lose your soul.

PRAYER

God, I want my life to be moving. I can't afford to navel gaze and wait for clear and absolute direction at every turn. If you have clear instructions you want me to follow, great, I'll take it. Otherwise, I'm going to trust what I know about You, and the situation You have put me in, is enough while I keep moving forward. Show me where I need to compromise and where I need to stand firm. Amen.

GET MOVING

1. What's the first unclear decision or unresolved conflict in your life that comes to mind right now?
2. Is there a compromise (that doesn't sacrifice

your commitment to Jesus) that you could make to help resolve the issue and move forward? Do it. Take the step today.

DAY 36

COMPETITION

When Peter saw him, he said to Jesus, "Lord, what about this man?" Jesus said to him, "If it is my will that he remain until I come, what is that to you? You follow me!"

- JOHN 21:21-22

IN THE GOSPELS, IT APPEARS THAT PETER AND JOHN are doing a lot of competing with each other. Both come from families whose business is fishing. Both are part of the original twelve disciples, and along with James, both are members of the inner circle of three to whom Jesus would give special time, teachings, and experiences.

When people have this much in common, they regularly become competitors. John has already established that he is the fastest one. He might have taken issue with Jesus saying that Simon's new name would be Peter, which means "rock," and that the Church would be built on his testimony. But Peter, too, may have been annoyed that John was "the beloved one."

Jesus is aware of this "sibling" rivalry. When Peter points to John, wondering if he is going to be treated fairly and equally, Jesus says, "I'll do whatever I want with him. Why do you care?!"

All of us have unique challenges and unique blessings in our life. Some of us have a knack with numbers, others with sales. Some of us have great parents, and others have a great wife. Some of us are very wealthy, and others are very healthy. We need to accept these God-given differences and make the most of what we have.

Competing with other believers is as fruitless as a dog chasing his tail. We need to be satisfied with the life we have and run in the lane God has placed us in, not look at people in different lanes to tell us whether we are winning or not. They have their race and you have yours.

PRAYER

Lord, I'm thankful for the life you have given me. I'm sorry for allowing the lives of others to rob me of contentment. That won't happen today. Amen.

GET MOVING

1. Identify someone in your life that you tend to compete with or envy.
2. Look for an opportunity today to encourage that person to their face.

DAY 37

MAKING ROOM FOR GOD TO MOVE

And they put forward two, Joseph called Barsabbas, who was also called Justus, and Matthias. And they prayed and said, "You, Lord, who know the hearts of all, show which one of these two you have chosen to take the place in this ministry and apostleship from which Judas turned aside to go to his own place." And they cast lots for them, and the lot fell on Matthias, and he was numbered with the eleven apostles.

- ACTS 1:23-26

I LIKE GOING TO VEGAS. I THINK THE TWELVE DISCIPLES would be with me on that.

In the passage above, the disciples are trying to replace Judas, who has just hanged himself after he betrayed Jesus. God never specifically told them to replace Judas, but there are plenty of good ideas that can be done without God giving clear directions. He hasn't given me clear directions to brush my teeth, but it's still a good idea.

Even though replacing Judas seems like a good idea, the way that the disciples do so may come as a shock. Personally, I'm not about to introduce games of chance into the equation as I hire a new employee or make other life decisions. But I'm still inspired by this move.

Casting lots is the disciples' way of giving God a voice and say in the process. It also ensures that the movement isn't bound purely by human planning and reasoning. Some of us have lives that are so planned out, God has no way to intervene other than crashing in with an overturned table, which can often bring pain. We need to slow down enough to give God space to insert Himself through means that we wouldn't expect. We need to be willing to take more chances—to gamble like the disciples did. In doing so, we are trusting God while wanting more than only we can generate in life.

PRAYER

Lord, I want the X factor of your presence in everything I do. Please make your presence and will known in the decisions of this day. Amen.

GET MOVING

1. If God wanted to show up right now and speak into your life, is there a place for Him to do it? How would you know what He's saying?
2. Take the next three to five minutes—especially if you've got an unclear decision to make—and sit quietly. (It's tougher than you'd think.) Just sit and wait. Give God space to speak, or at least space to give you an idea of how to resolve the issue. Who knows, maybe He'll have you flip a coin after all!

DAY 38

GROW GODLY AMBITION

Do nothing from selfish ambition or conceit, but in humility count others more significant than yourselves. Let each of you look not only to his own interests, but also to the interests of others.

- PHILIPPIANS 2:3-4

THIS VERSE TELLS US TO "DO NOTHING FROM SELFISH ambition," and we shouldn't. Having your own advancement as the only expressed goal of your life sounds a lot like selfish ambition to me. First and foremost, your life goals should be God's goals. Those should be the things that drive you most of all.

I'm not talking about living in a remote village with a loin cloth as your only earthly possession. Don't be so quick to assume that any goal that isn't hyper-spiritual is selfish. Ambition can be a good thing. Even a godly thing.

We need men to have the ambition to grow businesses that employ and feed a lot of people. We need men to have an ambition to be in long-term, committed relationships with their wives and children, influencing the next generation. We need men to have the ambition to be able to hear the voice of God and follow it. We need men to have the ambition to succeed in business, in relationships, and in spirituality.

We can learn so much about how our God relates to us when we consider how we relate to our kids. Do you want your child to be average? Do you want your child to earn just enough to put food on the table? No, you don't. And that's not what God wants for you either. To be clear, we need to be content with whatever comes our way, *and* we need to have an ambition that gets us up in the morning and gives clarity as to why we are doing what we are doing. The welfare of others is dependent on us having an ambition that surpasses just our needs.

PRAYER

God, I don't want to be average. I'm done with needing big numbers because it makes me feel better about myself. I'm also done with listening to the spiritual minimalists who believe that ambition is of the devil. You have placed things in my heart which I'm going to try to bring to reality while serving you. Amen.

GET MOVING

1. Are there any ambitions in your life right now that are clearly God ambitions? Things that are bigger than you by yourself could achieve? What keeps you from chasing them? Fear? Doubt? Worry?
2. Call a friend today to tell them about the ambition and say that it may have been something God gave you. Ask them to help you figure out a next step, and then do what they tell you.

DAY 39

PRE-QUALIFIED

Giving thanks to the Father, who has qualified you to share in the inheritance of the saints in light.

- COLOSSIANS 1:12

WE THINK OF BEING QUALIFIED AS HAVING THE RIGHT finances in order to get a loan. A bank's qualification is the result of the sum total of our previous financial practices. We get qualified purely based on how good we have been financially.

If I were a banker, I would operate the same way. You would only get what you have earned. Your past actions would be the sole determination of your future possibilities. Fortunately, God isn't a banker. Our past actions don't qualify or disqualify us for the life ahead of us: He does. He and He alone.

One time, I was ready to take the stage at an event and had a sick feeling that I wasn't spiritually qualified. The previous week I had committed some sins that I was sure would disqualify me from being used by God. Even though I had asked for forgiveness and repented, I was sure I had to re-earn God's trust in order to be qualified to talk about Him.

As I was wrestling with this feeling, the words of this passage in Colossians and the voice of God flooded my mind, as God said, "Brian, you don't qualify yourself. I qualify you, and I say you are qualified." God is saying the same thing to you. Don't disqualify yourself if God has already qualified you.

Live your day boldly and without shame over the things you've already confessed. Don't allow the Enemy to tell you that you can't speak up or step out. God needs you in the fight, and He says you are able.

PRAYER

God, there are too many things that govern the way the world works which I no longer want to govern the way our relationship works. I'm sorry for thinking that you operate on a normal, worldly level. Today I'll do what is before me and stop second guessing myself. Amen.

GET MOVING

1. God says that you are spiritually qualified to do what He's called you to do. Identify one thing that keeps you from feeling like you're qualified.
2. Share that thing with one person this week and ask them to pray for and encourage you.

DAY 40

WINNING IS A GODLY GOAL

Do you not know that in a race all the runners run, but only one receives the prize? So run that you may obtain it.

- 1 CORINTHIANS 9:24

DO YOU WANT TO WIN? I'M NOT ASKING YOU IF YOU want to be spiritual or if you want to be moral. I'm asking if you want to win. Life is not about participation. It is about winning. I can hear the weenie boys say, "But aren't we all winners?" No. There are some of us who win and some of us who lose. Some of us who maximize our potential and some of us who squander our potential. Winning doesn't have to mean hurting someone else's progress; it means maximizing the impact of your own life.

There is a lane that God has called each of us to run in. You are the only one who can run that race, and you must run it to win. In the next couple days, we will talk about ways you can accidentally disqualify yourself from your race. Religious people love that topic because it is a discussion of the rules. You can know and follow all the rules but not win. You can keep the Ten Commandments and not win. Every year, in my profession as a pastor, I'm confronted with the example of some other pastor who runs outside of his lane, breaks a commandment of God, and gets disqualified. I read those news stories with fear and trembling. I don't want that to happen to me, and if I focus on that fear, I might be able to avoid the same fate. But I want to do more than dodge failure. Who cares if no one writes articles about my mistakes if they also have no wins to write about?

Life isn't about keeping the rules. It is about winning. You have gifts, abilities, and opportunities no one else has, all of which have uniquely qualified you for the race you are in. God has given you one life to lead. He has given you this day only once to live. Lead and live in such a way that at the end, God will put a wreath around your neck and say, "Well done good and faithful servant. You won."

PRAYER

God, I'm sorry for only participating in life. I want to actually win in the arenas where you have placed me. Today I commit to go after things on my schedule so I feel the weight of a gold medal when I go to bed. Thank you for giving me a race to win. Amen.

GET MOVING

1. Make a list of the places you are winning and areas where you are losing.
2. Pick an area from each column. Identify one thing you need to keep doing so that you keep winning where you are winning and one thing you need to start in order to win where you are losing.

DAY 41

WINNING WHERE IT MATTERS

Every athlete exercises self-control in all things. They do it to receive a perishable wreath, but we an imperishable.

- 1 CORINTHIANS 9:25

THE APOSTLE PAUL WROTE THIS SECTION OF Scripture while imprisoned and watching the Isthmian Games. He saw athletes prepping for a competition they wanted to win, and it reminded him of his own race. If athletes deprive themselves of unhealthy things in hopes of having the Emperor put a perishable wreath around their necks, how much more should we be willing to go the extra mile in ensuring we live controlled lives that won't result in a far more significant DQ?

The spiritual life is not one of concepts and philosophies. Though it may sound contradictory, it is one of physical engagement. To be spiritual goes beyond doing spiritual things. To be Christian is more than controlling your financial expenditures. To be godly has higher aspirations than not masturbating while looking at an image of a woman you aren't married to.

To win means that we are nailing areas that matter. Do the people in your life want to be around you? Is your job trending toward outcomes that you are proud of and will be thankful for when you are on social security? Are you winning at home? When you look into your wife's eyes, do you see someone full of joy? Do your kids genuinely enjoy being around you?

Both atheists and believers can be world-class athletes. They will do what it takes to get their bodies to function at the highest level. They will forgo alcohol, tobacco, fried foods, or anything else that stands in the way of increased lung capacity and muscular strength. But it is only a believing man who will live with an eternal perspective under the gaze of a loving God. We want Him to look us in the eye at the end of life and say, "Well done!" I want to earn that imperishable crown mentioned in today's scripture passage. Throughout the Bible, God promises gifts and rewards to those who are faithful. I want those gifts and rewards and crowns. And so should you.

We need more men who will step out from the crowd and do whatever it takes to win the race God has placed them in. Be one of those men!

PRAYER

Lord, as I read this entry I am convicted about ____________. I'm sorry for that area of rebellion. Please forgive me. Today, I lace up my shoes to get back into the race you have called me to. Amen.

GET MOVING

1. Write "home," "work," "friends," and "personal care" in columns on a sheet of paper. In each of these areas, give yourself a gold, silver, or bronze medal. Don't give yourself any medal if you aren't on the stand at all.
2. Identify a workout regimen that will propel you toward a medal.

DAY 42

WINNING BETWEEN THE LINES

So I do not run aimlessly; I do not box as one beating the air. But I discipline my body and keep it under control, lest after preaching to others I myself should be disqualified.

- 1 CORINTHIANS 9:26-27

SOME PEOPLE BELIEVE THE CONCEPT OF WINNING IS unspiritual. Others have issues they never overcome which result in a DQ. But maybe the saddest group is the one who lives aimlessly because they don't know how to focus their lives. They live without winning in mind because they don't even know what that looks like.

The Apostle Paul, who wrote this passage, would see fighters shadowboxing while prepping for their bouts. Were they not to step immediately into the ring, this form of physical preparation would be meaningless. You punch a shadow to prepare you to punch an actual person. That is the aim of shadowboxing.

During my brief stint of boxing in high school, I learned there was a huge difference between training and stepping into the ring. Hitting a bag with perfect form doesn't mean you will ever land a punch against an actual opponent. You prepare and train so that you can compete and win. Training is controlled and predictable whereas competition is not. I think there are guys who are more in love with training than fighting and winning.

I know many guys at the gym where I workout who have very impressive physiques. Of course, just about anyone in the free weight section who is standing next to me looks impressive. As I've gotten to know a few of them, one thing is fairly common . . . they don't use their muscles outside of the weight room. Their carefully crafted workout wardrobe exhibits biceps that don't carry firewood, shoulders that never lift drywall buckets out of a pickup bed, and legs that don't squat down while camping in the woods. Muscles are for using in the real world, not displaying in our fabricated world.

In our spiritual lives, training looks like spiritual disciplines: reading the Bible, praying, going to church, etc. The fight, the competition, is to do the will of God as opposed to just practicing spiritual things. That will include things like reaching people with the grace and love of Jesus so that they can come into a relationship with Him. If we train without ever fighting or competing, then we are just building our "beauty muscles" while there are people who need help getting up.

There is a difference between playing to not lose and playing to win. The point of life is to know the One who has made us so we can be victorious in the ring He has placed before us and so that we can bring others to Him. Make no mistake about it, you are in a fight. There is an evil entity that wants to beat you. Don't let that happen.

PRAYER

God, I need to point my life in a direction which isn't aimless. I fight for you today. Amen.

GET MOVING

1. Is there an area in your life right now where

you're playing to win? Why is that? What's your motivation, and what sets your efforts and strategy apart from the normal person?

2. Now, with that in mind, think of an area where you're just aimlessly training rather than playing to win. Why is that? Take some of your focus, strategies, or discipline from the area where you're playing to win and apply them in this area today.

DAY 43

JESUS DOESN'T WANT YOU TO GET BEAT UP

Do not resist the one who is evil. But if anyone slaps you on the right cheek, turn to him the other also.

- MATTHEW 5:39

JESUS IS CLEAR IN TELLING US TO TURN THE OTHER cheek. But is it always to turn a physical cheek or is there something else going on?

Jesus is specific in calling out the right cheek. Getting struck on the right cheek is rare. Lefties make up only about 10 percent of the population. To hit a person's right cheek with a right hand requires a backhand. Jesus isn't talking about turning the other cheek when we are physically assaulted. He is talking about being verbally insulted. He is talking about being emotionally and spiritually resilient enough to not retaliate when we are mocked or taunted.

We are too quick to lash out on social media, on the highway, or at the dinner table. Ours is a generation of overly sensitive males who fly into road rage at the slightest offense. We vent our frustrations on social media as if someone else is listening or even cares what we are saying. So what if someone has a curt word for you? Who cares if someone whips you the finger in traffic?

Actually, I care. Receiving the finger from someone sitting in the safety of a car is an act of cowardice that gets me angry. But I remember to turn the other cheek. Let's resist that evil by not returning evil for evil.

Jesus is NOT telling us we shouldn't defend ourselves. If someone hits you, I hope you will protect yourself instead of thinking that Jesus wants you to have your skull fractured. If a foreign aggressor like Nazi Germany stands against the purposes of God in bringing death and violence, you better believe God wants someone to give a punch so that innocent lives are saved.

The big idea here is to be different. Following the ways of God will make us different from other people. We will shut up when others spout off, and we will step up when others step back. Let's do that today.

PRAYER

God, I thank you that I live in a peaceful time in a relatively peaceful country. I don't seek or welcome violence, but I will gladly lay my life down in a physical way in being the man I need to be. Amen.

GET MOVING

1. Purposefully seek to be rejected today. Go to a restaurant and ask for something not on the menu. Ask a stranger if you can have their dog. Give your boss a terrible idea and let her tell you "no." Build up emotional muscle for how to be resilient and reject being overly sensitive about your rejection.
2. Have you ever been wrongfully hurtful? If so, reach out to that person and apologize. Make it right *today*.

DAY 44

REPENT FOR REFRESHMENT

Repent therefore, and turn back, that your sins may be blotted out, that times of refreshing may come from the presence of the Lord, and that he may send the Christ appointed for you, Jesus . . .

- ACTS 3:19-20

MEN DON'T LIKE TO TURN AROUND. WE WOULD RATHER keep going forward and have our GPS reroute us than turn around and go the opposite way. Turning around can feel like admitting defeat. And yet, that's what true repentance is: turning from sin and going in a new direction.

One of the most beautiful motorcycle rides I've ever taken was at the White Rim Trail in Utah. It is all on dirt and borders a beautiful canyon rim. My friends still laugh at the horror on my face when, halfway through the route, at a rest stop, I realized the trail was a big circle taking us back to where we started. I proclaimed, "Men, our job is to get the #$%&

out of here!" I did not want to get stuck in a loop.

When we avoid repenting for our sins, we often get stuck in a loop of sin. We can easily become wearied by this loop because it doesn't offer the abundant life that God has for us. Repentance leads to "times of refreshing." When I'm feeling down or when life doesn't seem to be working, the first thing I do is a gut check on my walk with Jesus. Are there areas of rebellion in my life? Are there secret sins? Am I doing the things that I know God wants me to do?

When your tires are out of alignment with each other, the car will pull and shake. When your life is out of alignment with your God, the same thing happens. Things stop running smoothly, and there is tension that doesn't need to be there.

Of course, being down or having a life that isn't quite working does not always mean we are out of alignment with God. Sometimes life just sucks. But doing a life diagnostic is a simple first step to problem solving—simple because it is doable, but still potentially painful. Is there anything going on in your life right now that you would work with more seriousness to change if you knew you were getting hit by a bread truck tomorrow morning?

God wants times of refreshing to come our way.

This scripture is clear that those times will come when we change the direction of our lives, when we repent. We need the presence of the Lord in our day-to-day lives for this to happen. His presence blots out our sins. Not just functionally, but relationally with God.

PRAYER

Lord, refresh me today. I can't control you, but I can control my choices. Right now, I think you are tapping on my heart regarding ________________________ *. I want you more than I want that thing. I am changing my direction as of now. Amen.*

GET MOVING

1. Drive with your map app on today and intentionally miss a turn. Let it tell you to make a U-turn. Do it. That's an image of repentance.
2. That thing that God was tapping you on the heart about? Decide right now what you will do differently today to "turn around" and go the other way. Is it a change of routine?

Avoiding a situation? Having a difficult conversation? Whatever it is, do it in the next twenty-four hours.

DAY 45

ATTITUDE OF GRATITUDE

Who am I, O Lord God, and what is my house, that you have brought me thus far?

- 1 CHRONICLES 17:16

IN THIS PASSAGE, KING DAVID IS REFLECTING ON HOW far he has come. From the youngest and smallest of a band of brothers who no one took seriously, to a mighty leader of a mighty nation. He has attained military success, financial success, and familial success. He knows that what he has isn't only of his own doing.

I, too, have more than enough, and I'm still not thankful enough. I have more money than I ever thought I would have, and I still feel financial pressure. I have more people who are a part of the movement I'm leading, and I can still feel that things have stalled. I have written more books than I ever thought I would, and I still am unhappy that more people haven't read them. If ten years ago you had a picture of what your life would look like today, you probably would have said, "That looks great, I'll take it." But too often we are lacking an attitude of gratitude for all the things God has given us.

Depending on what shape you are in, your heart has beat fifty-ish times in the last minute and you have done nothing to earn it. God has spared you from mortal harm in the midst of all the stupid things you have done or that have happened to you. God has given you unique gifts and abilities. Reflecting on my countless blessings in life helps recalibrate me to gratitude.

As time marches on, we feel entitled to the blessings we have in our lives, and we forget the things God has done to bring us "thus far." We need an attitude of gratitude toward the things God has blessed us with. We need to stand back in recognition and reverence that God has taken us beyond our expectations. This is exactly how I feel.

PRAYER

Who am I, Lord God, that you have given me great health, a great family to love, great friends to live with, a great house to dwell in, a great mission to pursue, and multiple outlets for ministry and fun? I am not worthy. Who am I that you would give me the life I have?! Amen.

GET MOVING

1. Identify three things (relationships, possessions, opportunities, etc.) that God has blessed you with. Doesn't matter what they are, just that it's clear you couldn't have made them happen on your own.
2. Every time you see or think of one of them today, tell God a simple "Thank you." Every single time.

DAY 46

THE INSANITY OF RELIGIOSITY

"I saw a vision, something like a great sheet descending, being let down from heaven by its four corners, and it came down to me. Looking at it closely, I observed animals and beasts of prey and reptiles and birds of the air. And I heard a voice saying to me, 'Rise, Peter; kill and eat.' But I said, 'By no means, Lord; for nothing common or unclean has ever entered my mouth.' But the voice answered a second time from heaven, 'What God has made clean, do not call common.'"

- ACTS 11:5-9

JESUS AND ALL OF HIS FIRST DISCIPLES WERE Orthodox Jews who ate kosher. They followed the dietary laws that had governed their religion for thousands of years. Poor guys never got to experience bacon, let alone bacon-wrapped shrimp or deep-fried gator bites. When Peter has a vision of God lowering culinary items from the "do not eat" list, he proudly and habitually says, "no."

Peter has a religion that surpasses the will of God. God gives him a vision for what he can eat, and it doesn't live up to Peter's standards. High standards are a good thing. I wish more of us had them. But there is a fine line between high standards and living by religiosity. Religiosity keeps us from the life God wants us to have and actually stops us from doing the things God wants us to do.

My religiosity is a playbook which tells me what to do so that I can feel like a spiritual winner. Taking the time and energy to write this devotional was an opportunity that my religiosity wanted to say "no" to. My religiosity tells me to play it safe and to not take a risk in writing a devotional in a masculine voice. My religiosity is telling me to not touch or consume things that God doesn't really have strong opinions about like the Skoal that is between my teeth and gum right now.

The Bible is the ultimate standard of God's voice. It is very clear that being drunk is wrong. It is also clear in numerous instances that moderate alcohol consumption by someone who knows their limits is totally "kosher." It is insane that many religious people are known for being anti-alcohol or anti-dancing. The old joke has some truth: Why are religious people against smoking and drinking? It could lead to dancing.

Religion is a carefully constructed set of rules that tell you whether you are doing well or not. Oftentimes there is overlap between religion and the will of God, but this is not always the case. Peter's initial reaction is to maintain his dietary standards over the will of God. In this situation, it wasn't just going to affect his meals, it would affect who would be included in the Kingdom of God. At this point in church history, the institution was brand new, and the leaders of it were still wrestling with questions, like, should new adherents to the faith be forced to follow the old rules about food and sacrifices? Peter's food vision from God set the standard for allowing non-Jews into the Jesus movement. And, ultimately, it's why I'm here today. Thank God for Peter squashing that bug of religiosity.

PRAYER

Lord, I'm sorry for falling all too often into my rules and standards and not hearing from you. Forgive me for my judgmental and self-righteous ways. Help me to hear you and experience you this day. Amen.

GET MOVING

1. One of the easiest ways to tell whether we're following religion or following God is asking, "Where does this push me?" If a "rule" pushes me toward God, then it's probably from Him. If it pushes me toward more rules, or toward judging others, it's religion. Stop doing something for a week that you have always done but isn't necessarily from God.
2. Ask someone who really knows you well where they see religiosity in your life. Don't get hurt and angry when they answer your question. Instead, use it as food for thought as you learn to lean more into the freedom that God brings.

DOWNWARD MOBILITY

And while they were there, the time came for her to give birth. And she gave birth to her firstborn son and wrapped him in swaddling cloths and laid him in a manger, because there was no place for them in the inn.

- LUKE 2:6-7

JESUS WAS BORN A COMMON PERSON TO A COMMONLY impoverished family. "Swaddling cloths" has become a quaint Christmas phrase which keeps us from hearing what was really going on. Why did His parents swaddle Jesus with cloths? Because they didn't have a full-size blanket.

The Bible teaches that Jesus existed as God prior to His birth on earth. The God of glory who has always been wrapped in splendor is now wrapped in rags. I find it awe-inspiring that God would lower Himself for our sake, to take on a mission which would bring great pain to Him.

When is the last time you lowered yourself for a

mission? When is the last time you intentionally took a step backwards? When is the last time you willfully brought difficulty in your life because there was a vision worth inconveniencing yourself over? This is the kind of life that Jesus had and that He calls us to.

Why would He do this? Why should we? Because we have a vision for something better in the future which requires us to momentarily step backward and downward. God isn't against our advancement. He just has a different path which is tried and tested by all the spiritual greats.

PRAYER

Lord, I want to be different. I am about a bigger vision than having a comfortable day and a comfortable life. Today I commit to lowering myself to serve anyway I can. Amen.

GET MOVING

1. While you were praying, it's highly likely that God brought something to mind. (He tends to respond fairly quickly to prayers about hu-

mility.) Whatever He brought to mind—can you make it happen today? Within the next two hours? Something special happens in our lives when we reorient our lives around humbly serving others. God notices, and He shows up big time.

2. Show humility by looking for an opportunity to elevate someone else today. Maybe you give an unexpectedly large tip at the drive-thru window, or help clean up a mess in a public bathroom, or assist an elderly person or single mom at the grocery store. Look for the opportunity and seize it.

DAY 48

UPWARD ASSETS

And being found in human form, he humbled himself by becoming obedient to the point of death, even death on a cross. Therefore God has highly exalted him and bestowed on him the name that is above every name . . .

- PHILIPPIANS 2:8-9

GO TO A LOUD AND CROWDED PARTY OR THE CONCES-sion stand at halftime and shout "Bill" or "Janet" or "Mohammed" and no one will notice. But say the name "Jesus" and heads will turn. There will be an uncomfortable feeling as a hush falls on some people. This is because Jesus' name was exalted by His Father to be the greatest name of all time. It was a reward for the service He had performed in lowering Himself while being lifted on a cross.

There are some of us who have missions assigned to us which will have a tangible payoff in the next life but not this one. Others of us have missions which will pay off in this life but not in the next. Then there are those of us who will be blessed enough to receive rewards here and there.

One thing everyone who will receive rewards and blessings from God has in common: choosing a path that is initially difficult and humbling. Getting an education is difficult and humbling. Switching careers is difficult and humbling. Giving 10 percent of your income away is difficult and humbling. Continuing to do what you've always done is not difficult and humbling. It is the new challenges that force us to depend on God and step out in boldness.

The good news is that on the other side of downward mobility lies an invigorating life filled with rewards and blessings. If you have been through a long drought of blessings and you haven't felt that God has bestowed anything on you for a while, one place to start is by examining the choices you have been making. Lower yourself and start something difficult. Not just because it is what God wants you to do, but also because you will eventually get better things. Our God is a good rewarder.

PRAYER

Lord, today I want my eyes to be open to the possibilities that exist. I don't want to just see the difficult things, I want to do the difficult things. Please forgive me for being too short-sighted and not as interested as I should be in true rewards. I'm going to live for a better future starting now. Amen.

GET MOVING

1. Think about the last time you did something "difficult and humbling," or perhaps the last time you took on something new and unknown. How long ago was it?
2. Ask God to show you the new and difficult thing—even if it is simple—that He wants you to start. Now go and do it.

DAY 49

CLUELESS PRAYERS

For the eyes of the Lord are on the righteous, and his ears are open to their prayer. But the face of the Lord is against those who do evil.
- 1 PETER 3:12

I DON'T KNOW IF YOU HAVE NOTICED OR NOT, BUT I haven't been including any of the standard prayers that I hear people praying in public or in their devotionals. You won't find the standard altruistic, spiritual-sounding phrases here. Phrases like:

- Help me to be . . . (some form of a better person)
- Give me a desire for . . . (various good things)
- Please motivate me to . . . (do something I don't want to do)
- Give me discipline for . . . (stopping something I don't want to stop)

Those things are all good things to want, but prayer isn't the way we get them. I'm a fan of prayer. I devote multiple portions of every day to prayer. I know it leads to things that I can't do in and of my own power.

But you will never hear me pray for something I can and should do on my own. I've never prayed for the grass to get mowed. I've never prayed for muscle mass to be increased in my body. I've never prayed that God would magically bestow some character quality on me. Well, actually, I did pray for those things when I didn't have a clue because those are clueless prayers. God doesn't magically bestow us with the things we should be working toward—that would shortcut our growth and waste His time.

You can have discipline, but you are going to have to develop it one small decision at a time. You can be motivated, but you have to take the first few steps so that you can feel the benefits of working hard. Then you will have more motivation to do what you should do. You can have a desire for a pure sex life, but you will only attain it while saying "no" to some things and "yes" to others. Instead of the silly, useless, weenie boy prayers above, let's pray something like this . . .

PRAYER

Lord, I'm sorry for thinking that following you would be easy. Please forgive me for wanting the easy out and being unwilling to do what needs done. Today I'm going to start doing what I've only prayed and wished for. Thank you for giving me a mind to think with and a body to act with. Today I start to create the life I want instead of fantasizing about you just giving it to me. This day is yours. Amen.

GET MOVING

1. What's something you've been asking God for instead of working toward?
2. Tell someone about that goal and tell them to ask about your progress toward it one week from today. (That means you're gonna have to actually *do it*.)

DAY 50

THE POWER OF GUARDIAN ANGELS

The angel of the Lord encamps around those who fear him, and delivers them.

- PSALM 34:7

SOMETIMES THINGS WHICH SOUND TOO GOOD TO BE true are actually true. There is a Catholic Church down the street from me called Guardian Angel Parish. My Catholic friends would talk about guardian angels. This sounded as ridiculous to me as the tooth fairy: it would be great if it were true, but let's get real.

Turns out that it is true. I know this from multiple Bible verses (Acts 12:14-15, Matthew 18:10, Psalm 91:11) and from personal experience.

How many of us can recount times we should have died but didn't? I've been in numerous motorcycle accidents. I was nearly crushed by a school bus in third grade. Built tree houses high in the air in places that are far from OSHA-approved. Drove drunk many times in high school and couldn't remember how I got home. In college, I would shoot arrows high in the sky, out of sight, and a friend and I would then run around, holding an old door, and catch the arrows as they returned to earth.

Maybe guardian angels are the reason why we don't have more close calls than we do. We aren't to pray to angels. We are to go straight to God. Angels are God's servants, and they would be offended if we talked to them instead of the One they glorify.

Too many men refuse to believe that God offers protection. If we did believe that, we might take some more risks that could have great rewards. Tragedy will strike, pain will come our way, but not to the degree that the world says it will. Your life will be more meaningful if you step out from behind your airbags.

The Bible reminds us again and again not to take on a spirit of fear. This isn't just a command from God that we should honor. We should remember that God has also equipped us with angels who have our backs. What is it we are afraid of again? Why do we feel on our own and exposed? Why will we not make that bold move that is on our heart? God has called us and equipped us to live boldly in His service.

PRAYER

God, it is crazy that you are so mindful of my welfare that you have assigned a spirit to guard me. It is mind-blowing but also freeing. I don't want to waste your provision. No more playing it safe. I'm going to make a move to serve you today. Amen.

GET MOVING

1. What's an opportunity or obstacle that you're facing that terrifies you? God is very clear we aren't to be ruled by fear. Identify a next step you could take to overcome the thing you fear, then ask God to show up as you take that step today.
2. Think back to a time when you could (and maybe you should) have died. Take a moment to thank God for protecting and caring for you in that moment.

DAY 51

SOULMATES SUCK

Let your fountain be blessed, and rejoice in the wife of your youth . . .

- PROVERBS 5:18

LISTEN. I'M NOT SAYING THAT IF YOU HAVE A SOULMATE, she sucks. I'm saying that the very idea of soulmates is flawed. I've been married for thirty-two years, and if being happily married is dependent on having a soulmate, then I've done something wrong. If a marriage necessitates two soulmates who have an easy and always harmonious union, then I've been living a lie.

Anyone who has had a successful marriage for any length of time—and I would put mine in that category—will tell you that there are any number of people they could have built a satisfying marriage with. My wife, Lib, could have had tens of thousands of other guys who would have been at least as good as me.

I'm no thoroughbred. Even those people who marry the tip-top person of their dreams will eventually tell you that while spousal selection before the marriage is important, spousal activities while married is where the real game is.

I'm saddened that good men are passing on good women in hoping for a magical angel. I'm angry that deluded men are leaving good women for other women who are still just human beings. Marriage is amazing because you have a teammate who enables you to do what you couldn't do on your own.

Two trained horses pulling together will go beyond the sum of their individual abilities. They can actually pull three times as much. That is what marriage does: it helps us do more. But it even gets better the longer you are together. If the two horses have trained with each other over time, they can actually learn to pull four times what they could pull on their own.

Don't look for the perfect soulmate. Look for one you can pull with.

PRAYER

God, I want to be in a marriage that produces results beyond my individual abilities. Help me to see the good one you have placed under my nose and to do the right things with her. I am thankful for her and I want her to also go beyond her normal abilities. I commit myself to that task. Amen.

GET MOVING

1. If you're married, pick one simple way (that is outside of your normal routine) to serve and bless your wife today. Don't make a big deal out of it, and don't look for praise. Just bless her.
2. If you're single, what's standing between you and marriage? Make a move toward eliminating that barrier. For example, if you're not dating, then take a risk and ask someone to coffee or dinner this week.

DAY 52

THE GREATEST MIRACLE

And Jesus said to them, "A prophet is not without honor, except in his hometown and among his relatives and in his own household." And he could do no mighty work there, except that he laid his hands on a few sick people and healed them.

- MARK 6:4-5

WHEREVER JESUS WENT, THE GREATEST SHOW ON EARTH was happening. It wasn't just great teaching, it was true-blue miracles—blindness gone, demons cast out, the dead resurrected. We should expect God to do the unexpected. But when Jesus of Nazareth went to His hometown, they weren't impressed. They were too familiar with Jesus, having known Him since childhood, to go beyond the expected, and that kept significant, miraculous things from happening. A modicum of belief is required for acts of faith to take place.

Despite people's doubts and disbelief, Jesus still healed some sick people—a miracle and a mighty work if you ask me! This should be encouraging to us. If Jesus can miraculously heal the sick, even where people's faith is minimal, He can surely intervene in the direction our lives are taking, even when we may be doubtful. The greatest miracle God does is to take a life headed away from Him and turn it into one that is lived under His direction: a life where we give Jesus control, where He becomes our Lord and Savior.

We all want to experience physical miracles, but don't devalue the spiritual miracle of God having your heart. It is the greatest thing you will ever experience. It is the gateway to numerous mighty works, ranging from answered prayers to physical healings.

Christ died for you because He loved you. He still loves you. To make Him your life ambition puts you in rarefied air with all the spiritual greats of the past. You have the very Spirit that they had, which sets you up for a potent life. You are the mighty work of a miracle.

PRAYER

God, thank you for choosing me and changing me. It is a blessing I take for granted. I want to see great and miraculous things, but one thing I will always have is the work you have done and are doing in me. I praise you for that. Amen.

GET MOVING

1. Is there anywhere in your life where you take for granted what God has done in you?
2. Identify three different times today where you can stop to remember and thank God for the miracle He's done in your life. Mark them on your calendar or set an alarm for them right now so you don't forget.

DAY 53

THE POTENCY OF MALE LEADERSHIP

"Sirs, what must I do to be saved?" And they said, "Believe in the Lord Jesus, and you will be saved, you and your household." And they spoke the word of the Lord to him and to all who were in his house. And he took them the same hour of the night and washed their wounds; and he was baptized at once, he and all his family.

- ACTS 16:30-33

TWO MANLY APOSTLES ARE PAUL AND SILAS. THEY are thrown into prison for their faith, and then an earthquake rocks their cell, opening their doors and breaking their chains. For some reason they choose to stay. The Roman jailer, who will be blamed for those prisoners that do escape, is going to commit suicide as a result of dereliction of duty. When Paul and Silas tell him not to hurt himself because they have stayed, he gives his life to Christ. This Roman has such a transformational experience with God that he ends up leading his whole household to be transformed.

He wears his faith on his sleeve, and everyone follows suit and is baptized.

The best way to transform a culture is by transforming a family, and the most surefire way to see a family transformed is to start with the lead male. This includes long-term engagement with faith. A report by the Baptist Press indicates that if a child is the first person in a household to become a Christian, there is a 3.5% likelihood everyone else in the household will follow. If the mother is the first to become a Christian, there is a 17% probability. However, when the father is first, there is a 93% probability everyone else in the household will follow.[2]

I don't like the numbers, but the numbers don't lie, and neither does my anecdotal experience. The person who has the most spiritual impact is you. Women are generally much more spiritually healthy and spiritually driven than men, but men have a calling to lead their families to truth. The most potent thing in your family is you.

Father, I pray that more families around me would be trans-

formed. Bring a male into their households who can model what it looks like to know Christ. I know I'm the answer to that prayer for families in my sphere of influence. I welcome that role. Amen.

GET MOVING

1. What is one relationship (whether inside or outside your family) where God has clearly given you influence and potential impact?
2. Make plans today to connect with that person (face to face, if possible) within the next week.

DAY 54

AN UNDERRATED MAN

And her husband Joseph, being a just man and unwilling to put her to shame, resolved to divorce her quietly. But as he considered these things, behold, an angel of the Lord appeared to him in a dream, saying, "Joseph, son of David, do not fear to take Mary as your wife, for that which is conceived in her is from the Holy Spirit."

- MATTHEW 1:19-20

JESUS' MOTHER, MARY, GETS A LOT OF ATTENTION AT Christmas, and rightly so. If I were God, and I were going to place my son into the womb of a woman, I would choose the greatest woman available. Wouldn't you? But in our appropriate respect for Mary, many of us have inappropriately disrespected Joseph. We have ignored him and the role he had in redemptive history. Again, if I were God, I would want the best human stepdad possible for my son. Wouldn't you?

Maybe part of why Mary was chosen was that God knew that Jesus would have a strong and godly earthly father in Joseph. This passage says Joseph is a just man. Not a just person or adult, but a man. We need more just men in our world.

- A just man has a mind and heart to be considerate and deliberate in ensuring the right thing takes place.
- A just man endures while all the tangible signs look negative.
- A just man is patient for more data in waiting for a potential sign from God.
- A just man doesn't fly off the handle like a child when he is told that his bride is pregnant by someone else.

While Joseph is taking time to contemplate his next move, an angel appears to give him the low-down. With a better understanding of the stakes, he sets his mind to caring for Mary, and the rest is history.

Because Joseph is a manly man who hangs in during tough times, he gets to participate in God's story. That same dynamic happens with normal men like you and me when we patiently endure in the face of confusion and unexpected changes of plan.

PRAYER

Lord, I want to be a Joseph. As males all around me succumb to being average in letting their emotions and the difficulty of the present hinder their decision-making ability, I want to be different. Right now, I'm struggling with ___________________. I'm going to hang in there because what I'm hoping for is greater than what I'm bummed out by. Amen.

GET MOVING

1. Is there a place in your life right now where you feel like you're just hanging on? Where you're confused or at a loss for how to get up and keep going? It could be the thing you just prayed about; it also could be a career crisis, a family issue, a bad diagnosis, or something else.
2. Our first step to moving forward is understanding that we're not doing so in our own strength. Take a couple of minutes and ask God to show you other areas in your life where you can see hope and progress. It's never all

bad, so let Him remind you of where good is happening.

DAY 55

FIRST TO MARKET

Train up a child in the way he should go; even when he is old he will not depart from it.

- PROVERBS 22:6

IN BUSINESS, THE COMPANY THAT GETS THE PRODUCT first to market has a competitive advantage. It will take an inordinate amount of information to cause us to change our brand preferences. This is true in business because it is true in human development. The things we learn first will be our default OS. Parents should be first to market with key life information for our kids.

When my son was bathing as a child and playing with his wiener, I would say, "Do you know what that is? It is a penis." To my daughters I would say, "That is a vagina." I then described for them what would happen with these parts. All my kids had the same response . . . "Ewww!" It isn't weird to tell your kids about investing before they have a framework for understanding it. Nor should it be weird to tell them about sex before they can comprehend that gift of God. A good parent wants to set their kids up for future success by giving them early information.

Some guys are afraid to talk to their kids about sex. Here's the thing: for the rest of their lives, people will be talking to your kids about sex. There will be an unending sexual agenda that will be put in their face from friends, media, and other popular culture mouthpieces. You should be the first and most dominant voice that seeks to healthily shape your child's views on sex, money, God, and Chevy trucks. Your kids also need to hear your voice on topics like race, purpose, identity, and forgiveness. They need to know that you are for them in every way.

If you haven't done the right stuff in one of the areas above, it doesn't mean that you aren't qualified to speak into your child's life. If you got high regularly in the past and have stopped, you have a knowledge base that is personal, and you can lean on it. I accumulated massive credit card debt that I brought into my marriage. That didn't disqualify me from teaching finances to my kids, and I'm so thankful that they aren't saddled with the same mistakes I made.

Children are moldable creatures. And your purpose is to point them in the way they should go. They need you to do this. Our culture needs you to do this, and your God has equipped you for this purpose. Roll up your sleeves and get in the game. Be the first to market for your kids.

PRAYER

God, I'm more passionate about my kids' development than a corporation is about profit. I will not allow a less qualified person to form their mind and spirit. I want to be creative in getting your truth across. My heart is to bless them with something they can't yet fully understand. Thank you for parenting me. You are a good Heavenly Father. Amen.

GET MOVING

1. What is one area where you need to be first to market (or get to market) with your kids?
2. Tell someone (if you're married, it should be your spouse) about the conversation you

need to have—and then make time for it today. Don't wait.

DAY 56

THE GENEROSITY OF GOD

I gave you your master's house and your master's wives into your arms and gave you the house of Israel and of Judah. And if this were too little, I would add to you as much more. Why have you despised the word of the Lord, to do what is evil in his sight? You have struck down Uriah the Hittite with the sword and have taken his wife to be your wife and have killed him with the sword of the Ammonites.

- 2 SAMUEL 12:8-9

THESE WORDS COME TO KING DAVID AS HE IS BEING confronted for having had an adulterous affair. But that isn't all. He has had his friend, the husband of his lover, killed. There is no clearer way to say it: David has gotten caught in a perfect storm of his own making.

Through the prophet Nathan, God recounts some of the ways He has blessed David. Then He says the words, "And if this were too little . . ." and I start to cringe because I hear this through the lens of how I would power up on someone who had wronged me. I would say, "After all I've done for you. As if that weren't enough, you have to go and do awful things like this!" But God says, "As if this were too little . . ." (drum roll please) ". . . I would have given you more."

God would have given David *more*? I always think of God as stingy. I don't think of Him as wanting to bless me and be generous to me. My life hasn't been easy, and maybe your life has been even harder. Maybe you have gone for periods of time without food. Maybe you have slept out in the cold because you didn't have a roof. Maybe you have contracted a disease that has no cure. Maybe you can't name a single person who has been a help to your life. Maybe you have zero options for your future because there are no opportunities around you. Maybe you have no easy access to clean water.

For me, none of the things listed in the previous paragraph are true. I don't have loads of expendable income, nor a vacation house, but that list reminds me that God has been, and continues to be, good to me. Even if something from that list does describe you, it's still true that God has been generous to you in more ways than you realize or deserve. Maybe He's provided money from unseen places. Maybe He hasn't punished you for mistakes that deserved punishment. Maybe He has protected you from bad choices.

God isn't holding out on us. We all have blessings and some of us have a lot of blessings. I have more good stuff than bad to recount. That is because our God is generous. He isn't holding out on us. Some of us have a lot of blessings, and for some sick reason we think that means that at any moment God is going to say, "Hey . . . I forgot about Pete over there. It is time to serve him up a fart-infused sandwich."

No, your Heavenly Father has more to give you. You may not have it right now for a variety of reasons, but His heart is one of generosity. Isn't He good?!

PRAYER

God, I'm sorry for making you out to be like me or other unhealthy people in my life. You never tire of doing good. Let me just take some time and list out some things you have generously given me: __________________________ . Amen.

GET MOVING

1. Pick one of the things off your list of stuff that God has blessed you with and find some time in the next twenty-four hours to enjoy that thing. As you do, remember that this thing is a gift from God Himself, given to you for your joy.
2. We understand why God is generous when we feel the joy of generosity. Bless someone financially today. Buy their coffee. Pay for the person behind you in the drive-thru. Be creative.

DAY 57

WORKING FROM REST

Thus the heavens and the earth were finished, and all the host of them. And on the seventh day God finished his work that he had done, and he rested on the seventh day from all his work that he had done. So God blessed the seventh day and made it holy, because on it God rested from all his work that he had done in creation.

- GENESIS 2:1-3

"WORKING FOR THE WEEKEND" IS A FAMILIAR REFRAIN. IT almost sounds biblical because God basically worked for six days in Genesis 1 and then rested on His weekend. We are told to have a similar pattern in our lives. But there is one difference. God rested *from* His labor, while humans rest *for* the labor they are about to do.

We are sick and twisted people. We think we need to go into a day off or vacation gasping for breath or else we aren't worthy of the break. That kind of rest only gets us back to par. We need to be at par, like Adam and Eve, and then have rest which amps us for real productivity.

I have a neuroscientist friend who used to run the lab at the National Institute for Health. He said that the least productive people were those who logged the most hours. Those folks didn't have research breakthroughs or benefit science as a whole in any meaningful way. His theory is that they were too tired. He told me, "You got to shut down the circuits." If the brain keeps the chemicals flowing on the same channels without a break, then new neural patterns can't form—and new neural patterns are vital for the formation of new ideas.

It is when I'm getting off a motorcycle that I have a new idea. It is when I'm lying on a beach that I get a huge charge to get back to my day job. It is when I'm resting through working with my hands, which isn't my day job, that I get restored for staring at a computer screen and typing entries like this one.

You don't have to earn your rest from God. He isn't corporate America. He is your Heavenly Father who knows how this world and life work because He created this world and life. Do Him and you a favor: do something restful and do it soon.

PRAYER

Father, your ways amaze me. You are a good God to mandate that I rest. I thank you that you aren't a slave driver, but a father. I'm your son, and I need to do a better job of taking care of myself. Remind me when I slip into patterns of mindless activity that it is okay to rest. I also commit to rest in the next seven days by __________________________ . Amen.

GET MOVING

1. What's the thing that you just told God you'd do to rest? Put it on your calendar right now. Even better, invite someone to join you in it (unless of course that makes it stop being rest).
2. Where our money goes, so goes our heart. Spend money today on something that would facilitate rest and play.

DAY 58

SPIRITUAL SOCIALISM VS. SPIRITUAL CAPITALISM

The point is this: whoever sows sparingly will also reap sparingly, and whoever sows bountifully will also reap bountifully.

- 2 CORINTHIANS 9:6

A FRIEND OF MINE JUST GOT BACK FROM CUBA. I ASKED him how it was and he said, "Socialism doesn't work." Cuba is a land of mystery, rife with '57 Chevys and artistic architecture. At least that is how the magazines make it look. In reality, that's because it hasn't been possible to buy newer Chevys or newer anything in Cuba for decades. They have the old stuff because they don't have an economy that creates enough green stuff. Socialism is a great idea until someone else's money runs out. But that doesn't mean capitalism is God's gift to the world. We are all aware of some of the abuses and downsides that can come with the unfettered need for more. Still, the promise for more can lead to a promising future.

I don't get upset about economic socialism, but I do get upset about spiritual socialism—the belief that God should give equally to everyone regardless of what we do. That is not what the Bible says; the Bible says we reap what we sow.

People who believe in Karma believe that we will all eventually get what is coming to us. God is a generous being who gives blessings simply because it is in His nature and gives us grace that we don't deserve. But the idea of Karma isn't totally off base. God calls it "sowing and reaping." The decisions we make today will result in outcomes tomorrow. Negative and positive outcomes are in our future based on the seeds of action and inaction we are planting in our day-to-day lives.

- Getting used to being lazy at work? Get ready to be found out and fired.
- Serving your wife's needs? A fulfilling marriage is going to bring a lot of joy.
- Having a hard time disciplining your kids? Get ready for hell on earth when they turn sixteen.
- Sending thank you notes to those who buy

your product? You'll have a satisfied and faithful customer for a long time.

- Smoking a pack of cigarettes a day? You are going to have fewer days ahead.
- Hitting the gym regularly? Physical competency that enables you to experience more of life is yours to have.

Cast off spiritual socialism that trusts that good things are going to magically happen. Kill unfettered capitalism which is only fixated on a bonus that buys more boy toys. God wants your life to work and it works when you work on the things that will bring fulfilling joy.

PRAYER

God, thank you for being so generous, freely giving good things to me. Thank you as well for being a God that incentivizes me to go after what is best. I want more than shiny objects and sweet treats. I want a life full of things that are satisfying. Today I commit to work toward attaining things which will satisfy. Amen.

GET MOVING

1. Identify an area of your life—work, marriage, a friendship, physical health, etc.—where you're not actively "sowing" anything.
2. Decide on one way that you can start to invest in that area today. For example, if you want to invest in your physical health, you could carve out twenty minutes for some basic push-ups, sit-ups, and jogging around the block. No matter the area, start with something.

DAY 59

THE SPIRITUAL JONESES

Come to me, all who labor and are heavy laden, and I will give you rest. Take my yoke upon you, and learn from me, for I am gentle and lowly in heart, and you will find rest for your souls. For my yoke is easy, and my burden is light.

- MATTHEW 11:28-30

WE MEN DON'T LIKE TO LOOK FOOLISH. WE DON'T WANT to be the slowest in the class. We want to be seasoned veterans, not greenhorns. As a result, we tend to not try new things as we age. It is one thing hitting worm-burners off the tee when we are twelve, but doing so in a scramble at thirty-five is humiliating.

This physical reality is mirrored in the spiritual realm. Christianity seems to have so much knowledge associated with it that we feel that we can never get up to speed. We see some people who have been in the faith for a long time, and they have a way of life that seems totally foreign and unattainable. These observations are keeping many of us from being in spiritual growth mode.

This isn't unique to our time. In Jesus' day, the religious elite believed not only in the written law like the Ten Commandments, but also in the oral law which was passed down by rabbis. The oral law was full of unsubstantiated beliefs and practices. If you knew these things and practiced them, then you too could be a spiritual ninja.

The problem was that these things would weigh people down and keep others from giving God a try. Jesus says that His way is a light and easy way that brings rest. Not easy in the sense that there won't be difficulties, but easy in that it's *simple*. Don't get caught up in keeping up with hyper-spiritual people. You know enough to do things like love your neighbor as yourself. Following through on the things we know and understand is all you need to be one of the spiritual greats.

PRAYER

Jesus, I thank you for making life simple. I'm done trying to keep up with the spiritual Joneses. Today I'm going to put my head down and go forward on what I know. If you teach me more, great. I'm going to enjoy whatever light and simple things you have planned for me today. Amen.

GET MOVING

1. Gaining some new spiritual insight feels exciting, but we should be more focused on acting out what God has already taught us, because this leads to growth. What's something God has taught you that you're not yet really living out? The simpler, the better.
2. Look at your calendar today and decide the time and place that you're going to take your first swing at it. For example, if God is telling you to love your actual, physical neighbor, then put it on your calendar. Make space to go over, have a conversation, and see what happens. (Pro tip: bring him a beer.)

DAY 60

WEAPONS FOR DEFENSE

Then Simon Peter, having a sword, drew it and struck the high priest's servant and cut off his right ear. (The servant's name was Malchus.) So Jesus said to Peter, "Put your sword into its sheath; shall I not drink the cup that the Father has given me?"

- JOHN 18:10-11

I LIKE GUNS. THERE, I SAID IT, AND LIGHTNING HASN'T struck me dead. You don't have to like guns or own guns. Many manly men don't. But I prefer having a weapon that can be used in extreme circumstances, though I hope it will never come to that.

Peter used his weapon (in his case a sword) in a way that wasn't approved of by Jesus. His heart may have been in the right place—he was, after all, trying to drive his blade through the skull of a guy who was capturing Jesus to take Him to His death. But this was a death Jesus was embracing, so the show of force by Peter was ill-timed even though his intention to protect Jesus was honorable.

A sword isn't very concealable. Jesus would have seen Peter's sword ahead of time, but He never had Peter surrender it. I think it is a good thing for a man to be prepared. I think if you have a baseball bat hidden in your closet for an unwanted intruder, that may be a prudent move. At the very least, it gives a man a sense of security and preparedness.

Why have a section on weapons in a devotional? Because we don't forfeit our masculine need to protect simply because we follow Jesus. We know we need to financially protect people who are close to us. As a preacher, I'm trying to intellectually and spiritually protect people as I give them truth that keeps them from harm. Whenever we pray for someone, we are trying to spiritually protect them. To protect in every arena except the physical arena doesn't make sense. Just as we shouldn't neglect our financial and spiritual responsibilities, we shouldn't neglect our responsibility to protect.

Let's keep focusing on the spiritual disciplines like prayer and tithing but we better not ignore other base instincts that keep the right people alive. The la-la land assumption that all will be well if God is on my side is one of the things that keeps many men from taking Jesus seriously. You have a mind and an instinct for the preservation of innocent life. So does God.

PRAYER

God, thank you for not asking me to abandon common sense. I love the people you have put into my life. My commitment to them is real. I hope they never face physical violence. My preparation for that possibility though is no different than my preparation through various insurance policies; I am ready in case trouble comes. At the same time, I repent for undue fears I may have. You are my ultimate protector. Amen.

GET MOVING

1. No matter who you are or what your background, God has placed people around you for you to protect. This could be obvious (family or friends), or it could be a bit less so (younger team members at work that need an advocate, students you teach, etc.). Think through your day and identify one new step that you need to take to protect someone today. Then go and do it.

2. Think of a time in your life when you failed to be a protector. What caused that failure? Was it a lack of preparation? Fear? Confusion? Learn from this mistake to be better prepared for the future. And if you need to, apologize to the person you didn't protect well.

DAY 61

NOT EASY, BUT SIMPLE

But the Pharisees and the lawyers rejected the purpose of God for themselves.

- LUKE 7:30

IT'S BEEN SAID, "THE TWO GREATEST DAYS IN A MAN'S life are the day he is born and the day he knows why."

God has a purpose for your birth. Finding that purpose is incredibly important. It can be a process that is difficult and daunting. The key is to not be paralyzed as you search for the big purpose of your life. While they may not feel like world-changing actions, there are small things you can do every day that will put you in alignment with God, and that will help slowly bring clarity to the purpose question. They aren't easy, but they are simple. Things like:

- It isn't easy telling my wife I'm sorry, but it is

a simple action.

- It isn't easy balancing my personal budget, but it is a simple process.
- It isn't easy to give my employer my undivided attention when at work, but there are simple things I can do to ensure that happens.
- It isn't easy to get my body into shape, but there are simple things I can do every week that make it a reality.

In doing these small things with purpose, we build character, and through our character come opportunities for purpose.

The saddest thing regarding the religious people around Jesus' life wasn't that they had a hard time with Him, but that they rejected the purpose God had for them. May it never be said that "Brian Tome rejected God's purpose for him." And may it never be said of you either. What a sad thing it is to reject the purpose that God has for you. Are you in alignment with His purpose?

PRAYER

God, I want my life to matter, and for that to happen, I need to be aligned with your purpose. I don't want to say "no" to you, so today, while I have spiritual clarity, I say "yes." Yes to ______________________________ . Amen.

GET MOVING

1. Don't worry about what you don't yet know. What is one part of God's purpose for you that you *do* know?
2. Take a minute and think about your day. Is there one thing that isn't in alignment with that purpose? Do what you need to do to get that thing out of the way.

DAY 62

MAKING PEACE WITH PAIN

But Jews came from Antioch and Iconium, and having persuaded the crowds, they stoned Paul and dragged him out of the city, supposing that he was dead. But when the disciples gathered about him, he rose up and entered the city, and on the next day he went on with Barnabas to Derbe. When they had preached the gospel to that city and had made many disciples, they returned to Lystra and to Iconium and to Antioch, strengthening the souls of the disciples, encouraging them to continue in the faith, and saying that through many tribulations we must enter the kingdom of God.

- ACTS 14:19-22

PAUL IS LIVING HIS LIFE IN SUCH A WAY THAT PEOPLE are stirred up. Some are stirred to follow his God, and others are stirred to kill him. Old rabbinic writings from the first century reveal that the preferred method of stoning was to tie the victim's hands behind his back and his feet together. Then he was pushed face first off a platform twice his height. If he wasn't dead, they would drop a large stone on him. Whether it was this method or the method we more commonly imagine, throwing stones, it was way worse than the "stoned" some of us have experienced.

That Paul survives isn't what inspires me, though that is impressive. It is the fact that he went back to the same city that brought him such pain. I'm so tired of hearing from people about how hard life is and how they are questioning their faith. I'm so weary of people recounting the ways God has let them down as a reason to have doubts. I'm so sick of hearing whining and sniveling coming from grown men. Have you been bound and pushed face first off a ledge? Has anyone hurled stones at you in a way that has killed many people before you?

If the answer to those questions is "no," I don't even have to ask if you have gone back to the same city that nearly brought you to death for a second helping. Why did Paul do this? Because of his love for God. It is our love of God and other people which compels us to hang in there for another day. At the end of that day, we re-up for another day. This is the life I'm aspiring to live, and Paul inspires me to seek it.

I've been emotionally killed in the classroom. My whole life I've struggled with educational discipline. One day in church, out of nowhere, I got the strong sensation that God wanted me to go to seminary. My wife was in disbelief. At that point, I had yet to finish my four-year degree and I was on year seven. I had already taken Accounting 1 three times.

I was afraid of the pain of class, but I was more afraid of being disobedient to God. I made my peace with that pain, knocked off a class to finish my undergrad and enrolled in graduate theological work. What do you know? It went great. Finished my three-year degree in two and a half years with a 3.5 GPA. Sometimes the pain isn't as bad as we expect, but God is looking to see if we pass the test of making peace with the pain.

PRAYER

God, I'm sorry for being too easily discouraged. I know that when I quit is not when I'm at my best. I'm not being stoned, but I feel the pressure in ____________________ *. Help me to endure. Thank you for people like Paul who call me to a higher level. Amen.*

GET MOVING

1. Courage is not just going headfirst into the problems that we're facing. It's also being willing to call upon the team around us. Who is a teammate or brother in arms that you could call to help with the thing you're feeling pressure about?
2. Call them today. Even if it feels risky, uncomfortable, or awkward, do it. Uncomfortable is always better than alone.

DAY 63

RAISING YOUR HAND

Above him stood the seraphim. Each had six wings: with two he covered his face, and with two he covered his feet, and with two he flew. And one called to another and said: "Holy, holy, holy is the Lord of hosts; the whole earth is full of his glory!" . . . And I heard the voice of the Lord saying, "Whom shall I send, and who will go for us?" Then I said, "Here I am! Send me."

- ISAIAH 6:2-8

THIS MAY BE MY FAVORITE PASSAGE IN THE OLD TESTA-ment, if not in the whole Bible. I'm stirred by angels singing "holy, holy, holy." To be holy is to be distinct and set apart. And God is holy times three. He is in a category unto Himself.

Every day, God is doing things all around you. Every day, He is looking for a man to do His bidding. I'm not sure that He absolutely needs us, but He wants us. When my son "helped" me with projects around the house as a little tyke, it was his presence and willingness to be engaged that most touched my heart. I think your Heavenly Father feels the same way toward you.

I'm also moved by the question of "Whom can I send?" along with Isaiah's response. To this day I get an adrenaline spike and raise my hand to say, "Me! Please send me for whatever assignment you have!" There are things that won't get done until you step in and step up with a raised hand and feet that are quick to move.

When a man is about stepping up to the plate to handle problems, he is a rare man. He is a man who is distinct from the other passive males in our culture. He is a man who has been set apart for a life about others. This means he is holy and wholly engaged just like his God and just like Isaiah. Be one of those guys today.

PRAYER

Lord, you are a magnificent God in a category all by yourself. You are worthy of my praise, affection, and sacrifice. Whatever you have going on today, I want to be a part of it. Help me to notice what you want done, and I will do it. Send me! Amen.

GET MOVING

1. No matter your history or what you've done, today is a new day. It's a chance to raise your hand and volunteer for whatever God is doing. Are you willing? If so, tell God out loud that you're willing to follow Him today.
2. Get up and take a walk, just for a couple minutes, and ask God to show you *something* that He wants you to be a part of today. Tell Him you're willing and give Him the chance to show you.

DAY 64

THE ARMY OF THE DISCOURAGED

David departed from there and escaped to the cave of Adullam. And when his brothers and all his father's house heard it, they went down there to him. And everyone who was in distress, and everyone who was in debt, and everyone who was bitter in soul, gathered to him. And he became commander over them. And there were with him about four hundred men.

- 1 SAMUEL 22:1-2

MOST PEOPLE KNOW ABOUT DAVID THE GIANT SLAYER who took down Goliath. Few of us know him as the struggling man that ran for his life and dealt with discouragement. He has a lot of success as a young man, but then King Saul goes mad and chases him around in hopes of killing him. David isn't paranoid. But even if he was, just because you're paranoid doesn't mean they aren't out to get you (that's a line you can use again and again . . . you're welcome).

In the midst of his discouragement, this man who

is marked for leadership is hiding away in a cave. It is a cave which I've been to in Israel on more than one occasion. It is a stone hole that sits high on a hill. It is deep and dark, just like his mood.

People in the surrounding areas find out about his presence and start showing up en masse. While they are four hundred men strong, David's new army isn't going to strike fear in anyone. It is a group with serious issues. They are in distress, in debt, and in despair. However, these are the people who willingly choose him and the people who will eventually be blessed by him.

This is the state of Jesus' current army. Most of us are depressed or distressed or in debt or in despair. Why don't we have billionaires in our midst? Why are churches filled with hurting people? We normally come to God for the first time when we are at the end of our rope, not when we have the world by the tail. If you have problems and angst you are what is called . . . normal.

In reality few people have the world by the tail. It just looks that way. Your discouragement has been shared by men all over the world. You are not alone in your depression. You haven't been the first to be in debt. I've been right there with you. I had to live with my in-laws along with my brand-new bride the first year of our marriage due to high debt.

Hang on to your commander, Jesus. Your day of deep distress will eventually pass. It has for all of us. And when it does, you will have more perspective, gratitude, and strength for the life that is ahead of you.

PRAYER

Lord, I count myself among the hurting masses. I would be nothing and I would have nothing were I not an enlisted follower of yours. Please strengthen my fellow soldiers. Amen.

GET MOVING

1. Write down all the things right now that aren't going well in your life and are discouraging.
2. Write down all the things from the past that you were deeply in distress about. Notice that they have either passed or you have adjusted to a new normal and are doing fine. Use this as encouragement to apply to your first list.

DAY 65

YOU ARE LIKE GOD

So God created man in his own image, in the image of God he created him; male and female he created them.

- GENESIS 1:27

THERE IS SOMETHING SPECIAL ABOUT YOU. THIS ISN'T a boost-your-self-esteem entry where we all get participation trophies. I'm dead serious. There is something special about you. There are things about you which only God has. There are things about God which only you have. You are created in the image of God.

The happiness and mental health metrics of our country have been in steady decline. Maybe part of it is that more and more of us believe that we are a result of random chance—that there isn't a creator who has made you to be more valuable and important than any other breathing being. Maybe suicide is on the rise because our culture has done a really good job telling us that the rights of animals are equal to your rights. Or that random chance brought this universe into being, not a God who very well could have made the "big bang."

I love my dog Winston, and I like my cat Frank. But there is something special about real live people. Nothing other than humans can innovate and create. A beaver will never invent concrete. A fish will never figure out the laws of aerodynamics. No bird will ever figure out how to breathe underwater. As a human created in the image of God, you have unique capacities to create and conquer life.

Where there is a man aligned with God, there God is. If you are reading this before you go into your workday, understand that in your meetings, God is uniquely present because of *your* presence. You are like God, and this awareness *should* lift your self-esteem.

If you tell people that they are a random amalgamation of proteins enough times, maybe they start to believe it. Maybe they come to the logical conclusion that a life so difficult and pointless isn't worth living. NO! You are created in the image of God. He has you here because there are things that only you can do. Hang in there, brother. We need you. The world needs you, and God wants you.

PRAYER

Father, I'm tired of believing the stupid thoughts in our culture that keep me from seeing my worth. You have given me unique capacities, and I praise you for them. Today, I put them into practice. Amen.

GET MOVING

1. What's one thing you seem to have a unique knack for? Skills with a tool? A cool head in negotiations? A way with machines or spreadsheets?
2. Whatever thing came to mind, decide right now on one way you will unleash that unique capacity for God's Kingdom today.

DAY 66

ADVENTURE

Go therefore and make disciples of all nations, baptizing them in the name of the Father and of the Son and of the Holy Spirit . . .
- MATTHEW 28:19

IN THICK, OLD-SCHOOL PAPER BIBLES, THERE IS A SECtion in the back featuring maps of the missionary journeys of various apostles. Traveling around a region or even the world isn't a big deal for most of us. But in the ancient world, most people would die within ten miles of where they were born. For Jesus to expand His followers' vision to include the idea of going to distant places was for Him to encourage them to live lives of adventure.

We live in an adventure-starved world. We read about adventures, watch documentaries about them, and see pictures of other people's adventures, but few of us are doing things that stretch us beyond where we are comfortable. The first time I went to the Grand Canyon, I didn't have a GPS, and smartphones didn't yet exist. At breakfast, I asked our waitress in Flagstaff, the largest town near to the Grand Canyon, what the best route was, and she said, "I don't know. I've never been there." She had lived less than two hours from the Grand Canyon for her entire life, and yet she was missing out on an adventurous opportunity right under her nose—one that some people would even travel from different continents to experience.

What is on your calendar that will push you and open your mind up to new possibilities? What are you putting off doing because it freaks you out a little bit? What are you going to do that is going to require new skills? What thing makes you queasy but will also be wildly memorable ten years from now? These questions get to the heart of what adventure is.

Men, we are dying by papercut. Every day, things happen that take life from us. Every year, life grinds us down a little bit more. We need something that lifts up our head. Something that forces us to look off into the future. Something that, when we are done with it, raises our spirits to new heights.

You are not on earth to live a sane and civilized life. You are here to experience your God and to be enlisted on an adventure He has planned for you. Go do it!

PRAYER

God, I'm unsure of what adventure exactly looks like for me, but I am tired of being tired. I need to break out of the ruts that I'm in and follow an arrow to a distant place. Help me to see the steps I need to take. Amen.

GET MOVING

1. If you're searching for an on-ramp to adventure, don't start planning a trip around the world. What's a place where you could get outside of your normal ruts in the next two to three days?
2. Text a friend right now and invite them to join you. It will make the adventure sweeter, and it will keep you from backing out on yourself.

AFTERWORD

YOU DID IT. YOU READ AN ENTIRE BOOK IN AN AGE where many men don't read. Not only an entire book, but an entire book intended to move you to a new place spiritually. You are officially in the 1 percent.

Becoming more spiritually powerful isn't about accumulating more knowledge. It is about moving on the knowledge we possess. After sixty-six prompts of doing just that, I'm positive you are in a better place. Spiritual growth is a difficult process, not too unlike physical growth. Without tiny muscle tears that come from exertion, we can't get stronger.

It is likely you are feeling the spiritual, relational, and emotional benefits of completing this workout. You may also have some tearing in your life as a result of applying the content in this book. Some growth isn't so simple, nor completely pain free. But make no mistake about it: you are a better man now than you were before. Here's how to keep your momentum going . . .

1. The prompts in this book are great for male bonding. Find a group of guys to spiritually hang with who have similar strength goals. Introduce them to this content and put a regular spot on your calendar to do an activity together and talk about what you have read. Sometimes male conversation isn't the easiest to have, but these spiritual prompts are great discussion starters.
2. Have daily time with God where you read something from the Bible. When you come across a verse that seems to hit you, stop and reflect on it. Then do something that cements the learning. Growth isn't about quantity so much as quality.
3. Talk to God as you would a friend every day. He can take whatever you need to say. Tell Him how good He is and ask Him for things that are important to you.
4. Find a mission to throw your energy behind. When men have something we are doing with God, we end up needing and experiencing God in a profound way which just reading can't replicate.

If this book has worked for you it is because the content has been time-tested with thousands of guys I've shared it with. If you got something out of a good portion of these prompts, it is likely others in your sphere of influence will as well. I'm truly not trying to sell more books, but you introducing others to this content could be a mission God has called you to. We live in a world that is beating us down and trying to drive us away from God and each other. Stand against that agenda.

I'm excited about your future. God says in Jeremiah 29:11 that He has plans to prosper you. There is nothing more powerful than a man who is filled with the Holy Spirit and going the way of God. Your journey has just begun. You are a good man and I'm proud of you.

ENDNOTES

1 Wilkinson, Bruce. *The Prayer of Jabez: Breaking Through to the Blessed Life*. Multnomah, 2000.

2 House, Polly. "Want Your Church to Grow? Then Bring in the Men." Baptist Press. April 03, 2003. Accessed July 31, 2019. http://www.bpnews.net/15630/want-your-church-to-grow-then-bring-in-the-men.

Brian Tome is the founding and senior pastor of Crossroads Church, with campuses in multiple states reaching tens of thousands of people every weekend. Brian has authored four books including his previous best-seller, *The Five Marks of a Man* . He also hosts The Aggressive Life podcast. As an entrepreneur, Brian has opened several other non-profits and started Man Camp, a primitive weekend camping experience that has helped tens of thousands of men reclaim the code of manhood. An avid adventure motorcyclist and overlander, Brian camps more than 30 nights a year. He is married with three children, a son-in-law and a daughter-in-law, all who still like being around him. Brian lives in Cincinnati, Ohio.

WWW.BRIANTOME.COM

NOTES

NOTES

NOTES

NOTES

NOTES

NOTES

NOTES